Discipleship—
A Lifelong Spiritual Pilgrimage

Discipleship—
A Lifelong Spiritual Pilgrimage

A Disciple's Reflection on Actively Living in God's Kingdom Today

by Vernon T. Jones

RESOURCE *Publications* • Eugene, Oregon

DISCIPLESHIP—A LIFELONG SPIRITUAL PILGRIMAGE
A Disciple's Reflection on Actively Living in
God's Kingdom Today

Copyright © 2013 Vernon T. Jones. All rights reserved. Except for brief quotations in critical publications or reviews, no part of this book may be reproduced in any manner without prior written permission from the publisher. Write: Permissions, Wipf and Stock Publishers, 199 W. 8th Ave., Suite 3, Eugene, OR 97401.

Resource Publications
An Imprint of Wipf and Stock Publishers
199 W. 8th Ave., Suite 3
Eugene, OR 97401
www.wipfandstock.com

ISBN 13: 978-1-62032-944-3
Manufactured in the U.S.A.

The Scripture quotations contained herein are from the New Revised Standard Version Bible, copyright © 1989 by the Division of Christian Education of the National Council of the Churches of Christ in the U.S.A. Used by permission. All Rights reserved.

This book is dedicated to all of the faithful saints who have come before this moment in time and will come after, and who have attempted through their journey to follow and honor the Lord Jesus Christ. Some are well known, leaving behind practices and writings of great insight. However, there are also countless others, largely unheard of, who have certainly provided us with a wonderful foundation upon which we can build as we embark on our spiritual pilgrimage.

Contents

	Preface	ix
	Acknowledgments	xi
	Introduction	xv
ONE	Striving for the Kingdom of God—Repenting/Turning Around/Conversion	1
TWO	Striving for the Kingdom of God—Where We are Today	8
THREE	Prayer—How, What, and Why	18
FOUR	The Holy Spirit	31
FIVE	Discernment	43
SIX	Hope	54
SEVEN	Faith Equals Trust	66
EIGHT	Discipleship	75
	Bibliography	83
	For Additional Reading	85

Preface

Jesus commissioned the eleven, in Matthew 28, to go and make disciples of all nations. The word disciple is used quite frequently in the New Testament and refers to those who learn from and obey Jesus. In word and deed Jesus' life demonstrated what was required of those who wanted to imitate him. Jesus informs his closest followers in Matthew 6:33 about the importance of striving first for God's kingdom before anything else. Jesus outlines in Matthew 6:5–14 how and for what to pray. Additionally, while Jesus was in the garden of Gethsemane he went alone to pray as he often did and told those with him that they also needed to pray, Matthew 26:36–45. There are, of course, many more examples from Jesus' life that serve as models for us.

Jesus' teachings and actions clearly show what we should be doing to become lifelong disciples of Jesus Christ. Practices such as going away to a quiet place to reflect, praying, striving first for God's kingdom, and learning what the Scriptures tell us about following Jesus seem to be straight forward. However, it isn't that simple for many of us who want to become more intentional in our desire to grow spiritually. From my experience working as a spiritual consultant and a director of a small group ministry I quickly sensed the intense hunger of members of Christian

Preface

communities to learn more about spiritual practices. Those participants were seeking to learn more about their own faith journey, the basic steps to becoming a disciple of Jesus Christ, and some of the tools needed for that process.

Most of those people regularly attended worship services and were involved in various aspects of their faith community. However, they wanted to go deeper spiritually and therefore enthusiastically signed up for the classes that were offered. Some participants had a few ideas about what to do but they benefited from the discipleship concepts that I presented. A fair number from the classes formed small groups to aid in their continued pilgrimage. My role allowed me the privilege of walking with those seeking a fuller spiritual life.

Establishing disciplined practices in our highly scheduled, fast-paced society can often seem overwhelming to many today, let alone faithfully maintaining such rituals. This book offers some tools to enhance or to assist in starting this endeavor. Hopefully, regardless of your background, knowledge, or experience you'll find something of value in what is presented here.

It is my prayer that God's love and grace will fill your life through the Holy Spirit as you engage in your faith journey. May your spiritual pilgrimage strengthen your relationship with Jesus as you witness to and love those with whom your path intersects.

Acknowledgments

It is next to impossible to make a complete list of the people who have helped shape my life. It is equally difficult to acknowledge all those who had a hand in bringing this book to print. My heart is filled with gratitude to those mentioned here as well as many others who for limited space remain unnamed.

Some of the more obvious people to whom I am indebted are those who helped with the initial stages of this manuscript and gave meaningful support: Rev. Diane Greble, a Lutheran pastor (ELCA); Sister Christella Ritchey, the Order of the Sisters of Saint Frances; Sister Mary Anne Burkardt, the Order of the Sisters of Charity of Nazareth; and my son Kevin Jones, who is a freelance editor of documentary films, have all contributed to this process. Bishop John Schleicher of the North/West Lower Michigan Synod (ELCA) gave final draft feedback. I am also deeply grateful to my wife, Rev. Shirley Ross-Jones, a Lutheran pastor (ELCA), who read this manuscript and all of the supporting documents countless times. Her willingness to continue proofing and editing throughout this project, along with her encouragement were invaluable. For all of these people I am extremely thankful.

In addition to these sources of support there are other aspects of my life that helped to lay the foundation for who I am today and in reality have made huge contributions to

Acknowledgments

this book you now hold in your hands. In one's spiritual pilgrimage it is vitally important to be part of a faith community; in my life I have been formed and blessed by several.

Jerusalem Baptist Church in Youngstown, Ohio was the cradle where my faith formation began. My mother, who was a single parent, made sure that my brothers and I went to worship and Sunday school every week. As a young adult at Jerusalem I filled a number of different roles and began several spiritual habits that continue today.

While attending Youngstown State University I also became involved in its Campus Christian Fellowship. Being a part of this organization and others on campus enabled me to participate in an environment whereby people from different faiths, backgrounds, and cultures could come together in unity. That experience allowed me to be open to working, being in community, and becoming friends with a diverse group of people.

Following my marriage, St. Elizabeth Ann Seton Catholic Church in Pickerington, Ohio was the faith community that nurtured my family for a number of years. My late wife, Judy, was Catholic and we raised our children in that faith. I always attended church with my family and became involved in many different aspects of the community, but I never converted. However, my faith life grew and deepened there because of the loving and spiritual community that Seton was.

I later joined Epiphany Lutheran Church, also in Pickerington, where I once again became involved in various ministries. The communities of Epiphany and Seton were so supportive in getting me through the period when my late wife was under Hospice care. Epiphany and its pastor at that time, the late Rev. David Shugert, played a key role in helping me discern and answer a call to the seminary where

Acknowledgments

my life underwent several major changes over a short period of time.

Other faith communities that influenced this book were Bethany Lutheran Church in Louisville, Kentucky where I was their worship leader and spiritual consultant, as well as Christ Lutheran Church, also in Louisville, where I served as Director of Small Group Ministry. The two churches that Shirley has served have contributed to this process as well: St. Paul Lutheran Church in Louisville, Kentucky and St. Paul Lutheran Church in Alpena, Michigan.

There are many other aspects of my life that could be noted such as my time working in a steel mill, in the insurance industry (and the physical moves that career entailed), as well as all of my educational endeavors. Each of us is a compilation of all the life experiences and all the people we have encountered over the years.

Both Shirley and I lost spouses and that was very painful for us. However, both Judy and Shirley's late husband, Bob, will always be a part of who we are and will continue to influence how we live. I thank God for everything and everyone who has been and is a part of my ongoing life and spiritual pilgrimage.

Introduction

How This Book Came About

THE PURPOSE OF THIS book is to offer guidance to those who want to learn more about becoming a lifelong disciple of Jesus Christ. It will provide the tools to enhance or to help start your spiritual pilgrimage. The foundation for this book began when I was between nineteen and twenty years old, a young man with low self-esteem. I started reading self-help materials as a way to give my life direction and me a sense of self-worth. Those books were like manna for they filled a real need in me. After high school I worked in a steel mill in my hometown, Youngstown, Ohio. Those writings gave me a vision that was much larger than any provided by working in the mill or anything else in my environment.

Looking back those books were really very basic in nature. However, they generally gave a person, who was open to their concepts, some fundamental steps to take if one wanted to change his or her life or circumstances. They gave me some basic ways to improve my own self-image as well as providing me with a new way of viewing my life.

Some of the same concepts that the self-help publications gave to others and me are continued in this book.

Introduction

Practices like memorizing Bible verses, repeating positive-affirmation statements, having specific times of the day to repeat those statements, setting specific goals, becoming ready to make major changes in one's life, and being open to something beyond one's limited vision will be found within this book.

Of course I didn't know at that time that I would be where I am now and still be using those concepts and tools. However, we never know what skills or acquired knowledge will be called upon at some later time in our life. Those materials helped me to develop some disciplines, and ways of focusing on certain long-held beliefs and ideas. Those concepts are part of who I am today and are woven throughout this book.

These Concepts Continued and Expanded Upon

Becoming a more disciplined person allowed me to work in the mill full time, go to college part time, and eventually earn my bachelor's degree after eight years. In this book I talk about having a specific prayer time and taking a disciplined approach to my spiritual life. Establishing a specific time for certain tasks was necessary for me in order to work full time and take classes as well. This may sound really basic, but for me many years ago, it was a hard lesson to learn. But I did learn it and you will find this discipline outlined here.

After college and throughout my middle years my life was spent in the corporate world, allowing me to travel, live in a number of different locations, and have a wonderful family life as well. I continued reading self-help materials but over the years I also began reading books on spirituality. Things changed drastically for me after my late wife, Judy, had her second operation for brain tumors. During the last

Introduction

couple years of her life my world was turned upside down. Some of the self-help concepts and my business career became less important. Following Judy's time in hospice care and her eventual death, love, family, and relationships became more important to me; nothing else seemed to matter as much anymore.

I always considered myself a Christian who prayed and tried to do what God wanted of me, but those years sharpened my focus on striving first for God's kingdom. In this book you'll see how this became so important in my life and why it appears to me that anyone who wants to become a lifelong disciple of Jesus Christ should be open to looking toward God's will in their lives on a daily basis.

Because of this inner transformation, I was guided to leave my secular position and enter Trinity Lutheran Seminary. I went not knowing why, only that I was meant to go. The summer between my first and second year was one where I did a lot of reflecting about what God wanted me to do next. It came to me through prayer and meditation that I had what was needed in order to do what God wanted of me. In this book I'll talk about how the Holy Spirit gives us discernment, which comes out of our prayer life. In my own life and the lives of others whom I know, and in various authors whom I have read, there are many examples of discernment coming to us when we are open to God's direction.

How This Book Got to This Point

After receiving my Master of Theological Studies Degree from Trinity I became involved with various churches focusing on how God interacts in the lives of Christians based upon striving first for God's kingdom in our daily lives. This is the source of chapters 1 and 2 of this book.

Introduction

More recently I have worked for churches as a spiritual consultant and as a director of small group ministry. In those roles I was able to hold a number of classes and sessions on an assortment of topics and subjects. The participants in those groups had a desire to learn more about their own spirituality, what it means to be a disciple of Jesus Christ, and some of the tools needed for that walk. These classes also gave them encouragement and support for their pilgrimage. During those small groups and discipleship classes the pieces for the bulk of this book started coming together.

From a personal standpoint my own reading habits continued to change and I began reading more works written by both classic and modern spiritual mothers and fathers. Their insights became part of my own personal pilgrimage and are woven in and through this book.

This Book has Limits

As mentioned before, the purpose of this book is to offer guidance to those who want to learn how to become a lifelong disciple of Jesus Christ. It will provide you with the tools to enhance or to help start your spiritual pilgrimage. When I read those self-help publications they were something that I was hungry for and over time I became open to the changes they recommended. You, the reader, should approach what's presented here with an openness to change in order to benefit from the message outlined.

However, what this book cannot do is make anyone perfect or allow one to necessarily achieve some higher plane in the spiritual world. All of us are fallible human beings in God's earthly kingdom and will make mistakes, have good and bad days, suffer, and have pain, no matter how far we think we may have progressed on our spiritual

Introduction

pilgrimage. I pray that you will have an open mind and spirit to what is written here and ponder if and how it relates to you.

The Chapters

Each chapter can be viewed as a separate unit and can stand on its own and give the reader concepts helpful to their pilgrimage. Additionally, you will find a common thread woven throughout the entire book whereby the chapters build on each other and when taken together create a picture of some of the characteristics of an intentional disciple of Jesus Christ. Our pilgrimage starts with the most basic aspect of the Christian walk—that of conversion, which means turning away from the direction you're currently going and toward God's kingdom and will in your life. Next, we look at striving first for God's kingdom in our world today. There are so many distractions that can prevent us from doing this; being open to God's call takes effort and a willingness to take certain steps.

Looking at one's prayer life is the next area we cover, and it can be a very personal thing; however, in my opinion and that of many mystics and saints, prayer is one of the basic aspects of this spiritual pilgrimage. The chapter on the Holy Spirit hopefully will give you some insight into the role the Holy Spirit plays in this process. Discernment seems to be a natural outcome of a prayer life directed by the Holy Spirit. The frustrating thing about discernment is that it may not come when we want it or how we want it. Thus, talking about hope in the next chapter gives support and encouragement to carry on. From hope we look at how faith is synonymous with trust, believing that God will be with us on this walk, in the desert times and the

Introduction

mountain-top times. The last chapter talks about how discipleship is a lifelong pilgrimage.

Reader Interaction

However possible, you should attempt to become engaged in the spiritual process while reading this book and of course afterwards. When you receive insights, a new way of looking at things, or new clarity about some aspect of your walk, try to record and reflect on them. Rereading or reading the material slowly over a period of time may provide you with a more in-depth experience, than speed-reading it only once. There are questions at the end of each chapter for discussion and points for additional reflection. Meditate upon these questions and points either alone, with a prayer partner, or with a small group.

About the Book

I view this walk as a spiritual pilgrimage. A pilgrimage can be thought of as an ongoing journey to a sacred place. The purpose of this book is very direct and simple. It is written so that you the reader are given the tools and encouragement to strive to become the person that God wants you to be. If this book assists you on your spiritual pilgrimage then to God be the glory.

But strive first for the kingdom of God and his righteousness, and all these things will be given will be given to you as well. So do not worry about tomorrow, for tomorrow will bring worries of its own. Today's trouble is enough for today.

—MATTHEW 6:33–34

ONE

Striving for the Kingdom of God—Repenting/Turning Around/Conversion

Conversion, in other words, is a willingness to let go, to be led beyond where we are, to where we can be. . . . Conversion, then, demands self-discipline; it presumes struggle.[1]

—JOAN CHITTISTER

Turning Around

IN MATTHEW 3:2 JOHN the Baptist is telling those in the wilderness around Judea, "Repent, for the kingdom of heaven has come near." We have a similar message in Mark 1:14–15 where Jesus, after being baptized by John and then tempted in the wilderness, declares, "The time is fulfilled, and the kingdom of God has come near, repent, and believe in the good news." Both talk about repenting and the coming of the kingdom of God. Apparently, this was Jesus' first public statement. Also, John kept repeating that same message over and over again. Thus, the concepts regarding

1. Chittister, *Wisdom Distilled*, 144–45.

repenting and the kingdom of God seem to have been of great importance to both of them.

However, this wasn't the first time the need for repentance and facing toward God was mentioned in scripture. In Ezekiel 14:6–8 God wanted the house of Israel to turn their faces away from all their idols and turn toward God's face, which was set in front of them. This was a constant theme in other Old Testament writings as well, a message delivered by many sources other than Ezekiel. Finally, John and Jesus came delivering the same message.

Jesus' Message

During his three-year ministry Jesus taught by example, actions, and discourses how he wanted his closest followers to live after he returned to his Father. He taught them by how he prayed, how he treated the less fortunate of his time (like women and children), and how oftentimes God's ways would be opposed by the established political and religious structures. But, he initiated his public ministry by proclaiming the need to repent, for the kingdom of God was at hand.

As followers of Jesus Christ who desire to become more faithful disciples by starting or continuing a spiritual pilgrimage, it is easy to miss this first message of Jesus. Repenting, turning around, having a conversion, no matter how we state it—this is the first step on our walk. Conversion involves letting go of the past and requires self discipline and struggle. What is being talked about here is not a once in a lifetime event but a daily one. Diana Butler Bass writes about being "continually converted," recognizing that conversion is not a one-time event, but that "conversion is pilgrimage."[2] Thus, conversion is the first step of the spiritual pilgrimage to becoming a lifelong disciple.

To some this concept may be very familiar, but to others it may be an entirely new idea. This book's purpose is to give people tools to help them *begin* or *enhance* their spiritual pilgrimage. Before we can talk about prayer, Bible study, reflection, or any of the other things that we will address later, the concept of turning around must be addressed. In order for these spiritual practices to be meaningful, anyone who is committed to taking part in this walk should have as their focus God's will and God's kingdom in their lives, rather than the allure of the world.

The Challenge of Change

Many people in Christian churches are perfectly happy where they are and don't want to change or upset their comfortable world. However, Jesus was all about upsetting the status quo of his culture and the individual lives of the people he touched. He tells Nicodemus in John 3:1–8 about how one has to be born from above in order to see the kingdom of God. This of course caused a lot of confusion in Nicodemus' mind. Jesus wanted people to change and leave behind their old habits and ways of living. Butler Bass addresses this very point when she writes: "In the New Testament, Jesus asks everyone to change. With the exception of children, Jesus insists that every person he meets do something and change. The whole message of the Christian scripture is based on the idea of *metanoia*, the change of heart that happens when we meet God face-to-face.[3]"

---

2. Bass, *Christianity for the Rest of Us*, 65.
3. Ibid., 24.

Prayer will be covered in a later chapter, and it will be noted that prayer will change a person. Thus, if you don't want to change, leave prayer out of your life. In the same vein, if you don't want your existing world changed for the sake of the gospel and God's kingdom, then stay away from this aspect of the spiritual pilgrimage, because in the mind of scholars and in the Scriptures, conversion and repenting are a necessary part of the process. This means turning away from the old ways of living and turning toward God so that we return to the relationship that God wants for us. Some people are unwilling to do this because it will cause change in their lives, and they are afraid to let that happen. However, becoming a disciple, through repentance and conversion, causes change in our lives, and that is what this is all about.

Striving for God's Kingdom Today

The second part of this short message from John and Jesus was about God's kingdom. They both stated that the kingdom of God was near. If it is near, that must mean it is something people who want to follow their message should seek. Matthew 6:33 describes it as *striving* for the kingdom. The Apostle Paul takes a similar theme when he writes in Philippians 3:14, "I press on toward the goal for the prize of the heavenly call of God in Christ Jesus." How does striving or pressing for the kingdom relate to me in my Christian walk today? When we repent and strive first for the kingdom of God we are becoming the persons God wants us to be, in essence, more faithful disciples, for God wants to be in relationship with us.

Repenting/Turning Around/Conversion

Being Healed and Restored

We follow Jesus' words and actions so that we can be renewed by his love, not just for ourselves, but also for the sake of the world. Jesus physically healed the sick; however, a kind of healing just as important was one of an emotional or spiritual nature, allowing people to be accepted in their communities once again. He was bringing the kingdom of God near to those he touched. In trying to heal and save people, he was often challenged by the religious leaders who were always questioning him about why or how he could heal. In Matthew 12:22–28 he was accused of casting out demons in the name of Beelzebul, the ruler of the demons. But the Lord responded that a kingdom divided against itself could not stand; therefore he couldn't cast out demons in the name of the ruler of demons! He went on to state that if by the Spirit of God he could cast out demons, "then the kingdom of God has come to you." He healed people physically, but he also restored many to emotional and spiritual health bringing the kingdom to all those he touched.

This connection about being healed, restored, and experiencing the kingdom was written about by Ladd and Hagner: "When a person has been restored to fellowship with God, that person becomes God's child and the recipient of a new power, that of the Kingdom of God."[4] This concept of being restored could be a physical, emotional, or spiritual healing. It could also give us a peace of mind and spirit that we didn't have before our encounter with God's love through Jesus Christ. This new power/healing/peace/wholeness gives us the ability to continue on this walk, turning away from what we once knew, while always striving to face God's kingdom.

---

4. Ladd and Hagner, *A Theology of the New Testament*, 129.

Discipleship—A Lifelong Spiritual Pilgrimage

The Process of the Pilgrimage

The remaining chapters will focus on offering you some tools, examples to follow, and, hopefully, encouragement to help you on this walk. This process is different for everyone, for one size does not fit all. This sacred walk may seem easy and quick for some and long and hard for others. The most important thing is to start or continue with enhancements depending on where you currently are in your spiritual pilgrimage. But remember it all starts with conversion and striving first for God's kingdom.

Questions for Discussion

1. Do you have any baggage or distraction in your life that prevents you from becoming the person that God wants you to be? If so what is it, and how do you deal with it?

2. Does repenting seem to be an old-fashioned concept in today's modern world? If so, why is that?

3. How hard is it for you to change certain aspects in your personal life? Have you ever had to make any major life-changing decisions?

4. Is the concept of striving first for the kingdom of God a hard one to understand?

For Additional Reflection

- On a daily basis through prayer attempt (in the Lord's Prayer) to acknowledge your need for repentance.

Repenting/Turning Around/Conversion

- Read and reflect on the book of Jonah—a great story about how God forgives when we make any effort at all to repent, and that God is pleased when we do so.
- Meditate on Luke 15 about the joy in heaven over one person who repents.
- In twenty-five words or less write what you think God's purpose is in your life regarding striving first for God's kingdom and becoming a lifelong disciple of Jesus Christ.
- Reflect on the role that grace and the Holy Spirit play in making repentance possible.

TWO

Striving for the Kingdom of God—Where We are Today

Heaven [God's kingdom] is, consequently, as much now as it is to come, only yet to be in full. The more we sink into God, the more we immerse ourselves in goodness, the more we become the beauty around us—the more we transform evil into good, the more we love, the less we hate—the more we have of the heaven that is here, the closer we are to heaven forever. Heaven is not a place. Heaven is a process of growing fully into the fullness of Being.[1]

—JOAN CHITTISTER

Jesus' Message for Close Followers

IN MATTHEW 6:24–34, JESUS talked about striving first for the kingdom of God. This passage is part of the Sermon on the Mount that begins in Matthew 5:1–2a, "When Jesus saw the crowds, he went up the mountain; and after he sat down, his disciples came to him. He began to speak and

---

1. Chittister, *In Search of Belief*, 50.

taught them." Thus, what he was teaching about at that point was intended for those who were his closest followers, the ones who had made a commitment to him and his way of life. The message was for those who were willing to sink themselves more into God, to realize that this kingdom is here now, and that this new kingdom isn't a place but a process of becoming a close follower of Jesus Christ.

Therefore, when Jesus told them to not worry about tomorrow and to strive first for the kingdom, he was speaking to those who would become his lifelong disciples. This message applies to us today; we need to trust and follow the Lord Jesus Christ before we can attempt to live according to this challenging passage. This is intended for those who want to have a deeper relationship with Jesus but may not know the steps to make that happen. This chapter will relate how becoming a disciple in today's world involves striving first for the kingdom of God on our daily spiritual pilgrimage.

Why Did Jesus Talk about the Kingdom So Much?

Jesus talked about the kingdom more than any topic during his earthly ministry. He proclaimed that the kingdom of God was near. He wanted humans to repent, believe the good news, and turn toward God. When Jesus came into our world, God began to rule differently, and having the kingdom embodied in Jesus was evidence of it. Matthew 3:16–17 notes how unique Jesus' life and this kingdom would be. "And when Jesus had been baptized, just as he came up from the water, suddenly the heavens were opened to him and he saw the Spirit of God descending like a dove and alighting on him. And a voice from heaven said, 'This is my Son, the Beloved, with whom I am well pleased.'" There are several exciting and different things happening here

Discipleship—A Lifelong Spiritual Pilgrimage

that make this event the beginning of something entirely new. First, we have the heavens opening up; secondly, the Spirit of God came upon Jesus; and thirdly, the voice of God declared how special Jesus was. This new order was something about which Jesus wanted those around him to hear often. And what is this new order? Mitzi Minor states:

> God's eschatological activity in the world (i.e., drawing the basileia [kingdom] near) is underway even in the midst of the old ways that have not yet passed on. God's new age does not await a future, cataclysmic event to be launched—it has drawn near! Thus, Jesus proclaimed to the people of his day that they need no longer live under Caesar's rule, for the basileia of GOD is present and available for them![2]

Jesus wanted his disciples to know that God's kingdom was near or already here, that their actions and focus would consequently be different from the ways of the established religious leaders and the accepted practices at that time. If they wanted to be his lifelong disciples, they would travel a different path.

Striving First for God's Kingdom Needs to be Done First

In Matthew 6:33–34 Jesus tells his closest followers to strive first for the kingdom of God and God's righteousness before anything else. God's kingdom had to be their primary focus each day. Richard Foster talks about putting the kingdom of God first when he writes about the discipline of simplicity:

> The central point for the Discipline of simplicity is to seek the kingdom of God and the

2. Minor, *The Power of Mark's Story*, 18.

> righteousness of his kingdom first and then everything necessary will come in its proper order. It is impossible to overestimate the importance of Jesus' insight at this point. Everything hinges upon maintaining the 'first' thing as first. Nothing must come before the kingdom of God, including the desire for a simple life-style.[3]

No matter what else may call out to us on our daily walk, if we want to become more faithful disciples, striving first for God's kingdom must be our first priority.

Defining the Kingdom

When the phrase "the kingdom of God" is used one may get the view that this refers to a specific place or area that God rules. Thinking of the kingdom of God, however, in terms of rule or reign helps us realize it is not static, or confined to a set place. *Basileia* gives this concept a wider view and understanding than merely the kingdom. The rule or reign of God is anywhere God rules or where or when the will of God is being done.

In one of my seminary classes we had a guest speaker, a pastor, who participated in the early years of the civil rights movement in the south. I asked him if he could note any moments from his time with the movement that he thought showed evidence of God's kingdom. He stated that in one of the marches people of various races, religions, and ethnic backgrounds were all striving for a common purpose against one of the evils of society. He felt a bond and closeness to the people in the march that was unique and of a definite spiritual nature. He believed at that moment during the march he could sense God's kingdom in and around

---

3. Foster, *Celebration of Discipline*, 86.

the marchers. God's kingdom or *basileia* is anywhere God rules or reigns, where the will of God is being done.

We are finite people and can't fully describe God or God's kingdom in human terms. We aren't able to totally see or understand all that God wants us to be, or where God wants us to travel; however, we are asked to be faithful in our pilgrimage to keep on striving for the kingdom on a daily basis. Each day we must die to ourselves and be reborn into the kingdom. We empty ourselves to do God's will. At issue is taking the risk daily to strive for the kingdom.

As limited human beings, attempting to define the kingdom of God is a neverending challenge; thus, the key for us is to face God and God's righteousness and everything else will take care of itself.

Life Experiences

As we live in this world, grow, and mature we acquire talents and gifts along the way that will be used at a later time in our lives. God knows where we should be going and realizes what we will need when we get there, even though we don't! Let me repeat that—God knows where we should be going and realizes what we will need when we get there. Thus, if we are becoming the persons God wants us to be, then as we travel along this spiritual pilgrimage striving for the kingdom, we will acquire skills that only God knows when or how they will be used. Our role is to decide daily to keep on growing and walking.

Learning and Leaving

This pilgrimage is a process of learning and leaving. If we are striving for the kingdom, we are always learning things

Where We are Today

that will help us with our calling. This learning also involves leaving the old behind, for this life is a continuous process of death and rebirth. We leave what is behind to move to where God wants us to be. This leaving made possible by God's love for us, is done in love for God and God's people. In all of this, without love we have nothing, even if we think we are striving first for the kingdom of God in our lives.

Our Calling and Bringing God's Kingdom into the Present

"Once Jesus was asked by the Pharisees when the kingdom of God was coming and he answered, 'The kingdom of God is not coming with things that can be observed; nor will they say, 'Look, here it is!' or 'There it is!' For, in fact, the kingdom of God is among [NRSV footnote has *within* as an alternative] you'" (Luke 17:20–21). Jesus brought the kingdom near and among us into his time and into our time today. Because the kingdom is near to us today, one could note that there are many reasons God wants us to acquire talents and gifts on this pilgrimage. God has given us our talents and gifts God wants us to use, as they are needed for the kingdom that has already begun. We are *not* talking about doing good works in order to be saved. Rather, it is the activity that emerges from being justified by grace through faith. We do what God has called us to do on this side of the kingdom, because grace has filled our lives.

On this walk we are called to give up the *stuff* in our lives that God knows is holding us back from becoming the persons that God wants us to be, and so we can fulfill our call more fully. There will be pain and sorrow in this because we have to die to the old in order to be reborn to the new person God wants us to be.

Discipleship—A Lifelong Spiritual Pilgrimage

Minor wrote about the kingdom of God helping us to become the person God intends for us to be: "All the stories, including Mark's, tell us that the way to paradise, to the *basileia* of God, to being authentically human, goes through the wilderness. . . . Those who would be authentically human, therefore, open themselves in hope to the Spirit's guidance on the Way of the Lord to the *basileia* of God."[4] To be *authentically human* or the person that God intends for us to become requires traveling through the desert. In the desert times of our lives we acquire the life experiences that are most useful in this pilgrimage. When we are challenged, we mature by going through the struggle rather than around it. During this desert time we become more *authentically human* and more open to the guidance of the Holy Spirit, and we allow God to rule and reign in our lives.

We are All Going Somewhere

All of us are on a pilgrimage of some kind or another, no matter whether we are a part of a Christian community, just a visitor to one, or, in fact, *not* a part of any such community. We all are on an earthly walk on this side of God's kingdom that has already begun. Even if we believe we are just standing still and minding our own business, we are going somewhere. Either our travel takes us toward God, God's kingdom, and God's will in our lives, *or* away from God to something or someone else that takes the center stage in our lives.

---

4. Minor, *The Power of Mark's Story*, 25.

Choices

In deciding which way we are going, we also make daily choices. Often the easiest choice is to follow the direction and noise coming out of the secular world, because many around us are doing the same thing. But doing that may keep us from becoming the person that God wants us to be. What we do does affect God's kingdom here and now as well as how we advance on this pilgrimage. We often think that the choice we make may be too hard and the price too high. Thus, we often make life choices that many others will choose, because *if it is good enough for the Joneses it's good enough for me.*

Spiritual Pilgrimage and Striving for God's Kingdom Today

On the spiritual pilgrimage we are invited to make a choice that many refuse to make: the way of the cross of Jesus Christ. Choosing that road will make all the difference in our lives. Not that we will be perfect or better than anyone else, rather that Jesus Christ will be the Lord of our life. Roberta Bondi writes about living in God's kingdom:

> God's kingdom, which comes according to God's will, is a gift, not a nightmare of coercion. God desires our life and not our death. "Do you not realize," Jesus asks us, "that God's kingdom is where God's will is done and that God's will for you is for your well-being, and for the well-being of all God has created? This is the Kingdom you pray for. If you live in this awareness, then as far as it is possible in this world, you can live now in the Kingdom."[5]

5. Bondi, *A Place to Pray*, 61.

Discipleship—A Lifelong Spiritual Pilgrimage

On our spiritual pilgrimage we, as believers, are confronted daily with situations in life that tempt us and cause us to act one-way or the other. Even if we aren't looking for challenges, they nevertheless will come our way. Our role is to stay focused on God's kingdom and will and prevent these issues from blocking our path.

Discipleship requires commitment, and commitment is an accumulation of decisions that consistently support God's kingdom in the world today. What we do daily determines our path and definitely matters. Over time we can begin to see where the accumulation of our decisions and actions lead us and how it affects the kingdom.

When we strive for God's kingdom on this spiritual pilgrimage, set time aside to pray, and engage in Bible study and reflection, we are doing our part to bring about God's kingdom into this time and place as we become more faithful disciples.

Questions for Discussion

1. How is the kingdom of God being realized in our world today? Write down at least five specific areas.

2. In your life, how do your daily actions help move you toward striving for God's kingdom and will? What steps can be taken to become focused in this area?

3. In our society with all of its distractions, is it really possible to put striving for the kingdom of God *first* in your life? If so; what does it take?

Where We are Today

For Additional Reflection

- Over the next couple of weeks, intentionally look to see how God's kingdom and will are being carried out in you and those around you and record them in your journal.
- In your daily walk attempt to look at things through the lens of God's kingdom and try to strive first for the kingdom in your life.
- Jesus talked about the kingdom more than any topic during his earthly ministry. Read Matthew chapters 5–7, 13, and 18–20.
- This pilgrimage is also about learning and leaving. List a few things you have learned thus far in reading this book. List a few times you have had to leave things behind in order to continue becoming a more faithful disciple.

THREE

Prayer—How, What, and Why

"Prayer changes things," people say. It also changes us. The latter goal is the more imperative. The primary purpose of prayer is to bring us into such a life of communion with the Father that, by the power of the Spirit, we are increasingly conformed to the image of the Son. . . . None of us will keep up a life of prayer unless we are prepared to change.[1]

—RICHARD J. FOSTER

What is Prayer

SIMPLE PRAYER CAN BE defined as a two-way conversation between God and us; it opens us up to give and receive. There are many forms of prayer, such as intercessory prayer, contemplative prayer, and meditative prayer, etc.; however, we will focus on simple prayer. Simple prayer is the cornerstone of becoming a more faithful disciple on one's spiritual pilgrimage. How does one know that God walks, leads, and talks to us daily? Aided by the Holy Spirit

---

1. Foster, *Prayer*, 57.

Prayer—How, What, and Why

our prayer life can lead, guide, and comfort us. Jesus and the Scriptures have given us instructions on how, what, and why to pray.

We acknowledge that prayer, in addition to being the foundation for a lifelong disciple, will *change* us. If you don't want to be changed then don't pray! However, if we are serious about enhancing our spiritual pilgrimage then we will allow ourselves to become open to being changed by the power of the Holy Spirit. Joan Chittister writes, "The function of prayer is to change my own mind, to put on the mind of Christ, to enable grace to break into me."[2] This change will help us become the person that God wants us to be.

Prayer will cause us to become more like Christ. Through prayer we will be able to sense more of God's love and grace in our lives. That doesn't mean that we will have perfect lives; it does mean we will have assurance that no matter what this life brings, God's grace and love will always be with us.

Personal Prayer Life

Prayer has changed me and continues to do so as part of my pilgrimage. I believe that by prayer God has made me more of the person that God wants me to be. One of the things that should be very clear about my life is that I feel that what has happened to me is a Christian experience. I believe that by striving first for the kingdom of God and becoming a disciple of Jesus Christ that this has opened the door for situations that would not have happened without this experience.

---

2. Chittister, *Wisdom Distilled*, 35.

Discipleship—A Lifelong Spiritual Pilgrimage

I want to outline my prayer life, not to bare my inner soul or brag about what I do, but because I think it may be helpful for you, the reader, to know that I seek the guidance of God through the Holy Spirit on a daily basis and have learned that this guidance comes. My prayer life has evolved over many years, affects who I am, and what I do in the kingdom of God. My hope is that by outlining these practices you will be encouraged to either *start* or *enhance* your spiritual pilgrimage.

Taking Time to Pray

Having structured daily practices are extremely important on this pilgrimage. We can pray anytime during the day or night, but from Psalm 55:16–17 we are given specific instructions: "But I call upon God, and the Lord will save me. Evening and morning and at noon I utter my complaint and moan, and he will hear my voice." Morning, noon, and evening are times that are noted to pray. Desert mothers and fathers have practiced this routine for centuries with some monastic communities having more than seven times of prayer and worship in a day.

In this fast-paced world we may wonder how one can take time out of a busy day for prayer. But like anything else in our lives we will find time to do the things that are really important to us. Foster notes that "We must firmly discipline ourselves to a regular pattern of prayer. We cannot assume that time will somehow magically appear. We will never *have* time for prayer—we must *make* time."[3] Some of us may try and fool ourselves into believing that having a specific prayer time isn't important. But Jesus often went away to pray (Luke 6:12) and many renowned Christian

---

3. Foster, *Prayer*, 74.

leaders feel that it is important as well. Following Jesus' example seems like a good place to start our pilgrimage.

Morning Meditation

My initial morning meditation source is *Bread for the Journey* by Henri Nouwen. All of my prayer times start with the Lord's Prayer and then I pray for guidance for the day. There are a number of people, family members, and friends who are prayed for every day, which takes a few minutes. Following that, prayer is done in the Spirit. I then read and reflect using the morning prayer section of the *Book of Common Worship, Daily Prayer.* I generally read the Scriptures from the three-year Lutheran Liturgical Calendar for the upcoming Sunday. That way, when preaching, the Scriptures have an opportunity to sink into my spirit, and, if not preaching, they prepare me for taking part in worship later in the week. Reflecting in my journal and rereading a number of mantras that I've developed over the years concludes my morning prayer.

Most weeks my exercise routine includes jogging three days a week. During that time I pray as well, especially prayers for my family and close friends. Each week I select a Bible verse either from the Scriptures for the week or from a stack of Scriptures (on old business cards) that I have collected over the years. I memorize the Scripture and then repeat it as part of my jogging routine. Memorizing Bible verses is something that I have done most of my life, and it helps me cope with the challenges of life.

Discipleship—A Lifelong Spiritual Pilgrimage

Mantras

Mantras have helped shape my life as a disciple. These are repeated while jogging to keep me focused on God's will in my life. One mantra/prayer is "Let nothing disturb you, let nothing frighten you, all things will pass away except God; God alone is sufficient," (adapted from St. Teresa of Avila). This has helped me through some tough times in my life. Another saying that is repeated while jogging is "I believe I am always divinely guided. I believe I will always take the right turn of the road. I believe God will always make a way where there is no way." This last one was used at my former job in marketing in the insurance industry when traveling and visiting agencies. Before entering an agency I would say this as a way to help me handle whatever came up on the visit. These two centuries-old prayers have provided comfort and strength for me.

There are also two other prayers written by me, which I repeat. The first one: "Lord, help me get through this day, give me the wisdom for today, help me to enjoy this day. Because God is love, help me to love and be loved, and keep me from all spiritual and physical harm." I started a form of this prayer in 1996 when I thought that I would be losing my late wife, Judy, after her second operation to remove a brain tumor. At that time I was not prepared for the thought of her dying (we are never really ready) and was struggling with what the future held. I was going up to the hospital every day and not doing well at all. I realized that I couldn't deal with more then one day at a time. Thinking Judy might die at any moment was too much for me to handle; therefore, I asked God to help me make it through one day at a time after that operation. This was prayed so my mind could just focus on dealing with her recovery—one day at a time. I started saying that prayer then and kept it

Prayer—How, What, and Why

up even after she passed away. More was added to it as time went along to reflect other areas that needed to be prayed for in my life. This prayer reflects Matthew 6:33-34, as Jesus told his closest followers to just deal with one day at a time, striving first for the kingdom of God.

Discernment

I developed another prayer during the summer of 2001. I was between seminary terms and spent time reflecting and praying while trying to discern what God wanted me to do when I finished Trinity. I went to Trinity Lutheran Seminary in September 2000 not knowing why I was to go—only that I was led to do so. That summer during my reflection time I began praying, "Lord open my heart and mind so that I can see more of your vision for me, and become who you want me to be." Slowly direction began coming about my future. To this day I continue to use this prayer for God's guidance through the Holy Spirit in my life.

How and What to Pray

While we are on this spiritual pilgrimage, it is vital to understand that Jesus also gave guidance about how and what to pray. Believe me, I don't have all the answers and don't always get it right, but each day I have an opportunity to begin again.

> And whenever you pray, do not be like the hypocrites; for they love to stand and pray in the synagogues and at the street corners, so that they may be seen by others. Truly I tell you, they have received their reward. But whenever you pray, go into your room and shut the door and

> pray to your Father, who is in secret; and your Father who sees in secret will reward you. (Matthew 6:5–7)

Jesus goes on to give them the words of what is now known as the Lord's Prayer. It is the perfect prayer that covers all areas that would be needed in a prayer. It is used during many worship services across the Christian world, and many learn it as a small child. In my prayer practices it is used as well, and I would encourage any of you who want to start or enhance your spiritual practices to use it also.

How Jesus wants us to pray is noted in the quoted Scripture from Matthew. Basically it should be done where it doesn't draw attention to the one praying, but where all the glory goes to God. Henri Nouwen writes, "Jesus went to a lonely place to pray" and that is where Jesus heard from his Father. Nouwen went on to say, "A life without a lonely place, that is, a life without a quiet center, easily becomes destructive."[4] In this fast-paced society it seems important to have a lonely place or an inner-quiet center to be able to hear what the Holy Spirit is telling us.

My own personal prayer time is generally done in a bedroom when no one else is around. But I also have prayer times in an open church sanctuary and retreat centers. Each person should attempt to find what works best for them and their particular situation. Everyone needs to find that place or space where they can pray and listen in a quiet peaceful environment. The main thing is to start and try different things, and if one method doesn't work, try another way.

---

4. Nouwen, *Out of Solitude*, 25.

Prayer—How, What, and Why

Bible Verses

As noted before, I have memorized Bible verses to help me cope with the challenges of life. Usually the focus is on one verse a week in addition to my other Bible study. While traveling for my marketing job (before going to the seminary), I would write a verse on an old business card and then place it on my car dash. This helped me try to keep a positive attitude as I went from one agency visit to another. Sometimes one visit would be less than positive and I didn't want what happened to be carried over into the next call. Thus, these verses were there to help with my attitude. During this time I very seldom listened to the radio, but rather would pray.

These cards stayed on my dash whether or not a customer or work associate rode in my company car. One could say that it was a form of a witness because every once in a while someone would ask about the verse. Later on I would write Bible verses on a white board in my office for my support, but it also helped others who saw it. Thus, memorizing and reciting Bible verses are very much who I am and help me keep my focus on God's kingdom and this spiritual pilgrimage.

After jogging, or if getting ready for the day after my morning prayer time, another routine is done as well to help with my self-esteem and keep my mind on God. When shaving I repeat to myself Philippians 4:13, "I can do all things through Christ who strengthens me." This verse has probably helped me more than any other except for Matthew 6:33–34. I still see myself as that person with low self-esteem. Thus, this keeps my mind on knowing that my strength comes through Christ. When I take my shower, Romans 8:31b is repeated, "If God is for us, who is against us?" This is done for the same reason. While getting dressed the prayer, "Lord help get me through this day," is also repeated.

Midday Rituals

A midday prayer practice began while I was living in Buffalo, New York in 1989. My family and I moved there and within a short period it became clear that my work environment was a very negative one and required yet another move. My desire was to move back to central Ohio, so I started noontime prayers for guidance and discernment. At lunch instead of going to a restaurant or staying in the office, sometimes I would go to an open church sanctuary to reflect and pray. My family and I were able to leave that situation in 1990, but over the years this prayer discipline continued in one form or another. When at home I use the *Book of Common Worship*, *Daily Prayer* together with spontaneous prayer and journaling. Additionally, in most cities, Catholic churches are open during the day for prayer and reflection and so I generally do this once or twice a week.

Why Pray?

When Jesus was in the garden of Gethsemane before his arrest he gave a firm reason for praying:

> Then Jesus went with them to a place called Gethsemane; and he said to his disciples, "Sit here while I go over there and pray." He took with him Peter and the two sons of Zebedee, and began to be grieved and agitated. Then he said to them, "I am deeply grieved, even to death; remain here, and stay awake with me." And going a little farther, he threw himself on the ground and prayed, "My Father, if it is possible, let this

cup pass from me, yet not what I want but what you want." Then he came to the disciples and found them sleeping; and he said to Peter, "So could you not stay awake with me one hour? Stay awake and pray that you may not come into the time of trial; the spirit indeed is willing, but the flesh is weak." (Matthew 26:36–41)

We pray because we are fallible human beings and will have trials on our earthly travels. We pray because we may have good intentions, but may not have a willing spirit to walk the right path, for we are weak and sinful people who need comfort and guidance on this spiritual pilgrimage. E. Stanley Jones is quoted as saying; "When prayer fades out, power fades out. We are as spiritual as we are prayerful; no more, no less."[5] If you want to have a spiritual essence on this pilgrimage, regular prayer is needed to nourish and enrich your spiritual being. At one of the low points in my life I was feeling weary and started an evening prayer practice to help deal with a difficult task that I was facing.

Evening Periods

Before going to bed I pray for an extended time during weekdays. This evening routine started when my late wife, Judy, was in a nursing home recovering from her second operation. She was there for about five weeks after spending seven weeks in two other hospitals. My son was with her during the day, and after working until mid-afternoon each day I would go to the nursing home to be with her. We realized that she received better care if someone was there with her, thus we made a point to always have one of us there. In the evenings I was unhappy about leaving her to

5. Jones, "Conversion," 303.

go home, so I used a *Christ in the Home* booklet and started reading it with Scripture and prayer before leaving her each night. After she came home and had learned to read again, we each did a part every evening before going to bed.

When Judy went under hospice care we continued to do the evening prayer and reading until she passed away. Afterwards I continued, and it has evolved a lot since Judy's death. My time begins with relaxing my mind and spirit and then praying the Lord's Prayer. I still use the *Christ in the Home* booklet, read the Scripture for the day, and then pray for my family and friends as well as praying in the Spirit. After that I read some other Scripture passages that are important to me. Portions from 1 John 4 about God being love are then read. After Judy died, I missed being loved by her, and this passage assisted in my healing and helped me focus on God's love. Other Scriptures that have helped me stay focused in areas that need constant reinforcement in my spiritual pilgrimage are also read: Matthew 6:19–34, Lamentations 3:21–26, and Habakkuk 2:2–3. In addition I read a few pages from a spiritual book, then I end this time by writing in my journal.

Additional Practices

Recently retreats have become a part of my life, either at retreat centers or at another location where part of my time can be used in a self-directed retreat. During these self-directed retreats part of the day is always spent reflecting in a church worship space.

In addition to the above, my wife Shirley and I pray together as a couple before leaving in the morning. We take turns every day praying aloud for our family, our community, the world, and for each other. This practice has enriched our spiritual and married lives.

God's Guidance

It is hard for me to think of any other way to live in this world other than having some type of prayer, Bible study discipline, and reflection. From my standpoint and belief God definitely guides and directs us through the Holy Spirit. I daily ask God to help, change, and guide me and then look to God to do it. Thus, in all of the events of my life, whether it was in losing a spouse, moving to a new job or city, answering a call to the seminary, meeting someone to share the rest of my life with, or dealing with family challenges, God in the presence of the Holy Spirit was and is there.

Questions for Discussion

1. Is the Lord's Prayer out of date with our times?
2. Prayer has been defined in many ways; how would you define it? How has that view changed over time?
3. Have you ever used forms of prayer other then simple prayer? If so, which ones and how did they help you?
4. Do you agree with the reasons given for how, what, and why to pray? If not, why not?

For Additional Reflection

- Attempt to set a specific daily time and place for prayer, Bible study, and reflection, no matter how short, long, or involved it is. Think of committing to start this ritual in some fashion, or enhance your current practice if already started.

Discipleship—A Lifelong Spiritual Pilgrimage

- If you don't already have one, think of getting an easy-to-read study Bible, the NRSV, NIV, or some other modern translations are options. For other books to read and meditate on see the "For Additional Reading" list at the end of this book.
- Think of journaling as a way to reflect upon what you are going through.
- At some point in your pilgrimage consider purchasing a devotional to give more structure if needed. There are many to choose from. One that I have used is the *Book of Common Worship, Daily Prayer* published by Westminster John Knox.
- Reflect on the many passages about prayer, in addition to the ones in this chapter. Begin with James 5:13–20, Matthew 7:1–12, and Jeremiah 29:10–14.

FOUR

The Holy Spirit

The Holy Spirit of God, the third member of the Trinity, himself accompanies us in our prayers. When we stumble over our words, the Spirit straightens out the syntax. When we pray with muddy motives, the Spirit purifies the stream. When we see through a glass darkly, the Spirit adjusts and focuses what we are asking until it corresponds to the will of God. The point is that we do not have to have everything perfect when we pray. The Spirit reshapes, refines, and reinterprets our feeble, ego-driven prayers. We can rest in this work of the Spirit on our behalf.[1]

—RICHARD J. FOSTER

Prayer and the Holy Spirit

SIMPLE PRAYER IS THE basic cornerstone of any spiritual pilgrimage. Without consistent, focused, and humble prayer all of our remaining efforts could be misplaced. This spiritual pilgrimage is one where we are striving for the kingdom of God using the disciplines of prayer, Bible

1. Foster, *Prayer*, 98–99.

study, and reflection. All of this is to become more faithful disciples and the persons God wants us to be. The Holy Spirit is part of our pilgrimage because of the role the Spirit plays in our prayer life. The Holy Spirit can be more of a mystery than our knowledge or lack of knowledge about God, the Father, and Jesus Christ.

No Perfect Prayers

The Holy Spirit walks with us in our prayers. The Spirit clears up what we have a hard time expressing, and corrects those things that need fixing. As fallible human beings we make mistakes in our moment-to-moment existence. This includes our prayer life in that we often miss the spiritual mark; but when we do, we shouldn't stop praying, or stress out because it isn't perfect. The Holy Spirit will bring the prayer to where it needs to be. We do our part in the process by praying sincerely and with a humble heart. In Paul's letter to the Christians in Rome he addresses this very topic: "Likewise the Spirit helps us in our weakness; for we do not know how to pray as we ought, but that very Spirit intercedes with sighs too deep for words. And God, who searches the heart, knows what is the mind of the Spirit, because the Spirit intercedes for the saints according to the will of God," (Romans 8:26–27). The Holy Spirit has been given to help us in our prayer life especially when we are not sure for what we should be praying. God knows the heart of all of us and uses the Spirit to intercede for us. We can't fully grasp the workings of the Holy Spirit in regards to our prayer life, we believe that the Spirit works in our striving for God's kingdom, maybe not in our time frame and maybe not in the fashion we want or desire.

The Holy Spirit Helps Us See Things in the Light of God

The Spirit helps us see the kingdom of God in this time and place. The Spirit does not take us away from the everyday joys and sorrows of life, but does help us navigate through them. Thomas Merton wrote about how this aspect functions in our walk: "If we pray 'in the Spirit' we are certainly not running away from life, negating visible reality in order to 'see God.' For 'the Spirit of the Lord has filled the whole earth.' Prayer does not blind us to the world, but it transforms our vision of the world and makes us see it . . . in the light of God.[2] Prayer will cause us to look at all aspects of life with a different set of lenses; that is, we will see the world in the light of God. When our focus is on striving for God's kingdom, we will not only see things differently, but what is important to us will change over time. How we react toward certain events and actions in the world will come to reflect this new set of lenses through which we are now looking at things in life. When the Holy Spirit guides our prayer life, the Spirit will not only direct us, but also cause us to look at things, as God wants us to see them.

Why Have We Received the Holy Spirit?

The Holy Spirit, the third Person of the Trinity, has a vital role on this pilgrimage; thus, having a better understanding of what the Scriptures tell us about the Holy Spirit is important. Therefore, we will start at the beginning of the book of Acts.

> While staying with them, he [Jesus] ordered them not to leave Jerusalem, but to wait there

---

2. Merton, *Contemplative Prayer*, 112.

Discipleship—A Lifelong Spiritual Pilgrimage

> for the promise of the Father. "This," he said, "is what you have heard from me; for John baptized with water, but you will be baptized with the Holy Spirit not many days from now. . . . But you will receive power when the Holy Spirit has come upon you; and you will be my witnesses in Jerusalem, in all Judea and Samaria, and to the ends of the earth." (Acts 1:4–5, 8)

The Holy Spirit came to give us *power*. Jesus had ascended and his disciples were going to need something to help them carry on the mission that Jesus gave them. Often I have mentioned that even when we strive first for God's kingdom and engage in spiritual rituals, we still have pain and sorrow and our lives will not be perfect. Jesus knew sending his followers out to the ends of the earth to be his witnesses would require more strength than they had as mere mortals. They needed the power, support, guidance, and boldness that this unique gift of the Holy Spirit provided.

Even though some of those disciples had been with Jesus for three years observing what he did, listening to what he said, and being in his presence, they needed something more to become witnesses to the ends of the earth. Because they waited together as instructed, they received what Jesus had promised to empower them for witnessing.

In the same way we need the power of the Holy Spirit before we can move into the space where we can continue becoming lifelong disciples and effectively do the ministry to which God is calling us. I believe the Holy Spirit is a gift given to every believer by God, and like God's love, is with us all the time. However, this gift is like a muscle in our body that grows weak when it isn't used. It needs to be exercised and used daily in order for all of us to reach our full potential. In our spiritual pilgrimage it seems important to

The Holy Spirit

seek the guidance of the Holy Spirit as Jesus did and become fully open to the Spirit's power.

The Coming of the Holy Spirit

On Pentecost, the Holy Spirit came upon the disciples after the ascension of Jesus. The coming of the Holy Spirit was foretold by Jesus, John the Baptist, and by the prophets in the Old Testament. "When the day of Pentecost had come, they were all together in one place. And suddenly from heaven there came a sound like the rush of a violent wind, and it filled the entire house where they were sitting. Divided tongues, as of fire, appeared among them, and a tongue rested on each of them. All of them were filled with the Holy Spirit and began to speak in other languages, as the Spirit gave them ability," (Acts 2:1–4). The story about the coming of the Holy Spirit is an exciting one. If you haven't read Acts 2 and reflected on it, I would encourage you to do so. What happened on that day hadn't occurred before and the eye-witness reports are quite amazing. To hear others speaking in many languages simultaneously, and to experience the power present must have been awesome.

Filled with the Holy Spirit

Another amazing thing that happened was that the house was *filled* and they were all *filled with* the Holy Spirit. Why did this happen? Because they did what Jesus told them to do; they were together as a community and they were all waiting and praying. (Acts 1:14a reads "All these were constantly devoting themselves to prayer.") Think about that for a moment, they were completely surrounded with and totally filled up by the Holy Spirit because they did what

Jesus told them to do: they were together as a community and they were praying.

When something or someone is filled with anything, there isn't any room for something else. In this case since they were completely surrounded with and filled up by God's Holy Spirit and for that moment in time there wasn't any room for their own agenda, their own selfish motives, any hateful thoughts or actions, or things of the world. They were compelled to follow the spiritual path as directed by the Holy Spirit. Relating this story to our pilgrimage shows that we too can be filled with the Holy Spirit and become more faithful disciples when we pray in the spirit of the early followers. The Holy Spirit came for them and comes to us today.

We receive the Holy Spirit in our baptism as noted in Titus 3:5–8 and outlined in the Small Catechism by Martin Luther, a "bath of the new birth in the Holy Spirit."[3] Truly we are the receivers of this precious gift upon our baptism, but the Spirit continues to be received throughout our spiritual pilgrimage.

What the Holy Spirit Provides

> I believe that by my own understanding or strength I cannot believe in Jesus Christ my Lord or come to him, but instead the Holy Spirit has called me through the gospel, enlightened me with his gifts, made me holy and kept me in the true faith, just as he calls, gathers, enlightens, and makes holy the whole Christian church on earth and keeps it with Jesus Christ in the one common, true faith.[4]

3. Luther, "The Small Catechism," 359.
4. Ibid., 355.

The Holy Spirit

The Holy Spirit does a lot of things for and to us. However, one of the key things the Spirit does is make us holy. Being made holy, consecrated to God, is a process just as we have been talking about spiritual pilgrimage as a process. It doesn't happen in one instant, or at some exact moment in time. This endeavor involves a lifetime of striving for God's kingdom on a daily basis and engaging in spiritual practices.

Our relationship with God changes us as we open ourselves through prayer to receive this gift from God through the Holy Spirit. On our spiritual pilgrimage we can't do it all by ourselves, but as Luther has written, the Holy Spirit calls us through the gospel and helps us believe in Jesus and come to him. We can see the Father through the Son by means of the Holy Spirit.

Characteristics of the Holy Spirit

In Matthew 3:11–12 John the Baptist notes that Jesus will baptize with the Holy Spirit and fire, and Jesus will take his winnowing folk, gather the wheat into the granary, and burn the chaff with an unquenchable fire. A winnowing folk was used to throw the wheat into the air so the wind could blow the chaff away. John notes that Jesus will burn the chaff with an unquenchable fire. Therefore, when one is baptized with the Holy Spirit and fire, the facets of our being and behaviors that are no longer needed will be burned away. Thus, the aspects of one's existence that run counter to God's kingdom and that of becoming a lifelong disciple will be removed by the Holy Spirit.

In the Old Testament Joel 2:28 states that the Lord will pour out God's spirit on all flesh, and there will be prophecy, dreams, and visions. Now just because we are on this spiritual pilgrimage doesn't mean that we will start prophesying or having visions. We could, but it doesn't necessarily mean that we will begin to do so. However, I believe what it does mean is that we will begin to have a different vision of life. We will begin to see things in the light of God. Our focus and the way we approach our daily life will change and our view will become more focused on God's kingdom rather than upon our own agenda.

In John 14:26 Jesus tells his followers that the Holy Spirit will come from the Father in Jesus' name to teach them everything and to remind them of all that was told to them. The Gospel stories portray Jesus' disciples as often misunderstanding what Jesus was trying to do. I can still remember a seminary professor stating numerous times: "*The disciples just didn't get it!*" Jesus knew that they needed the Holy Spirit to teach and remind them about what Jesus had told them. The same holds true for us today: we need the Holy Spirit to help teach us and to constantly remind us of what Jesus has done.

Every day that we wake up we are a new creation. By God's grace we look at life differently and react to life's happenings through a new lens. We need the daily teaching of the Holy Spirit to keep us turned toward God's kingdom versus ending up on another path. In John 16:12–14, Jesus mentions to the disciples that the Holy Spirit will guide them into all *truth*. "I [Jesus] still have many things to say to you, but you cannot bear them now. When the Spirit of truth comes, he will guide you into all the truth; for he will not speak on his own, but will speak whatever he hears, and he will declare to you the things that are to come. He will glorify me, because he will take what is mine and declare it to you."

Just because a pastor says something doesn't mean that it is God's truth, and just because we hear something from a public figure doesn't mean it is God's truth. God's

The Holy Spirit

truth is hard to discern in our society today because of the many voices bombarding us each day with conflicting messages. Often we don't know who to believe. Jesus said that the Holy Spirit will guide us in all the truth, for the Holy Spirit will not be speaking on the Spirit's own, but to glorify Jesus. When we hear messages, we can ask, who is the message bringing glory to, to the speaker or to Jesus? *The Holy Spirit will direct us to truth by guiding us to Jesus and God's kingdom.*

The Holy Spirit and Guidance in My Life

The Holy Spirit comes to make us holy and also to comfort and guide us. Being open to this Spirit is vitally important as we strive for God's kingdom. An example of this for me was when the idea of going to Trinity Lutheran Seminary came to me. In following the Spirit I received a wonderful surprise. Getting to know, fall in love with, and marry my wife could have only happened because both of us have tried to follow the guidance of the Holy Spirit in our daily walks. Remarkably, we both arrived at Trinity at the same time. I came to Trinity not knowing why I was going; I only knew that this was what God wanted me to do. This guidance came in a number of ways and it was apparent that I was meant to be at Trinity in the fall of 2000. My initial thought was to work full time for one more year and go part time for the first year and start full time in 2001. Up to that point I had spent twenty-seven years in the insurance industry and was very comfortable there and could have stayed longer. Also, Shirley's pastor at the time tried to get her to go to Trinity in 1999. This wasn't what she was intending to do either. If she had started earlier and if I had gone part time (probably in the evenings) we would never have met and eventually married in 2002.

Discipleship—A Lifelong Spiritual Pilgrimage

One of the things that allowed me to go full time happened through my pastor. Once when he and I were talking about me going to Trinity and possibly going part time, he asked me how much it would cost for one year: I told him, and he said to let him see what he could do. Later on he told me what had happened. He prayed about my situation and the name of a couple from our church came to him. He went to visit them and explained who I was (for they did not know me) and what I was planning. His hope was that they might give some part of the tuition for my first year at Trinity. He then planned to go to others in our church to see if he could get the remaining amount. He said that he had never done anything like that before but was guided to do so. That couple called him back, and amazingly, they promised to pay the entire first year's fees, books, and tuition. Wow! That told me that I was meant to go full time and not wait.

What a wonderful thing to have happened to me! They also provided for my second year's expenses as well. God through the Holy Spirit does direct us in all aspects of our lives when we're striving for God's kingdom. Shirley and I wouldn't have met if we had attended Trinity at different times. Yes, I believe God divinely guides all those who seek God's will.

The Holy Spirit on this Spiritual Pilgrimage

When we are receptive to the guidance of the Holy Spirit, the Spirit will form us as Jesus was formed and will open us up to a world beyond anything that we can see at the present time. "As Jesus responded to the Spirit in his own life, so we realize can we. As Jesus was formed by it, so we now

The Holy Spirit

know are we. . . . The Spirit opened Jesus to a world beyond his own. The Spirit does the same for us.[5]

In classes that I have led related to this pilgrimage, I have used the image of the globe. Picture yourself on the equator of this globe and each day you wake up you move an inch or so around it. Every day you see something different from what you saw the day before, the angle and what is seen change daily. In the same way, I feel that when you are on your spiritual pilgrimage, striving for God's kingdom and taking part in spiritual practices, each moment, each hour, and each day the Holy Spirit will form you and open up the world to you in a new way, never before seen. Each day your angle or view of life changes and things appear that you weren't able to see before. This all starts with simply beginning the trip. The Holy Spirit will come and walk with you and provide guidance and discernment as needed for the next step.

Questions for Discussion

1. According to Romans 8:26–27 the Holy Spirit helps us with our prayers. Does that sound possible to you? List your reasons either way.

2. Acts 2 describes the Holy Spirit coming to the community. To your knowledge, has something like that ever happened since?

3. The Holy Spirit comes to make us holy. On this spiritual pilgrimage do you think this can happen to you or someone you know? If so, list what these changes would look like.

---

5. Chittister, *In Search*, 88.

Discipleship—A Lifelong Spiritual Pilgrimage

For Additional Reflection

- In your daily walk be open to the guidance of the Holy Spirit on this pilgrimage and in seeing things in the light of God.
- Read and reflect on Acts 2 and the coming of the Holy Spirit to the community of believers. This is an exciting story and goes on to tell how the Holy Spirit gave direction to this early community.
- Look at how the characteristics of the Holy Spirit apply to you, as it relates to where you are today and to where God might be leading you in the future.
- Picture yourself on the equator of a globe and meditate upon how your vision of this life pilgrimage has changed over time.

FIVE

Discernment

Discernment . . . is a perilous practice that involves self-criticism, questions, and risk—and it often redirects our lives. . . . In emerging Christianity, discernment is the spiritual process through which *metanoia,* being "born again" in God's truth, beauty, and love, occurs. . . . For centuries, discernment has been understood as the way of spiritual maturity.[1]

—DIANA BUTLER BASS

As WE TALKED ABOUT in the last chapter, the Holy Spirit always walks with us along our spiritual pilgrimage. The Holy Spirit provides the guidance and discernment required for the next step along the path. While working in the property and casualty insurance industry for more than twenty-seven years, most of my time there was involved in marketing and business planning. The analyzing of future business writings was something that took time, foresight, and lots of research. Often the plans written were for six months, one year, three years, or even longer. Of course nothing was ever static and changes or adjustments were frequently made along the way.

1. Butler Bass, *Christianity for the Rest of Us,* 95, 97.

Discipleship—A Lifelong Spiritual Pilgrimage

Long-term planning is not often done, however, in spiritual pilgrimages or in the spiritual practices of prayer, Bible study, and reflection. My experience on this walk has been that most often only the next step appears. Christian discernment is definitely unlike the structured planning found in the modern business world.

Discernment Comes through Prayer

The discernment from the Holy Spirit that comes through prayer follows the guidance given in Matthew 6:33–34 that states that we should focus on today and not be concerned about the worries of tomorrow. In other words we are to strive for God's kingdom today and trust God for tomorrow.

This type of discernment is often difficult for those on this pilgrimage to accept because everywhere we turn people are focused on their careers, their lifestyles, and the modern pressures of life. Trusting God for discernment and direction is a situation of definitely swimming against the current in this stream called life. Most of us would rather *not* take it a day at a time because that leaves too many unknowns and uncertainties about what is to come.

Discernment is Part of the Process of Change

Christian discernment carries with it risk and will redirect one's life. If you haven't gotten the message about this spiritual pilgrimage yet, here it is again: *it will change and redirect your life!* You can't get around it or sugarcoat it. You will be changed and see life through a new set of lenses. Change is something that Joan Chittister also has some strong words about:

Discernment

> THERE IS NO SUCH THING, social scientists know now, as "controlled change." Change is a dynamic that builds a coherent future out of a chaotic present. Change, if it is real, takes us where we have not been before and could never have imagined that we'd go. It takes the courage of an explorer, the fancy of a dreamer. The process is simple: there is either control or change. You can't have it both ways.[2]

This pilgrimage will take us to places that we haven't even thought about, both physically and spiritually. We need to have courage and be open to what God may be doing in our lives. Trying to maintain a static life is not possible once one has become fully engaged in this spiritual pilgrimage. The discernment we receive during this process will change and redirect our lives.

Discernment is a spiritual process, something we never get to the end of, something we engage anew every day. ("Discernment: The process of assessing and evaluating, particularly in relation to trying to determine God's will in a particular situation or for one's life direction."[3]) That "assessing and evaluating" is part of our daily pilgrimage.

Discernment and Patience

This process of determining God's will in our life may often frustrate us: I know that it does for me. By nature I am not a patient person. For part of my life my thinking was that if a person planned and thought situations through and then worked hard at those plans, things would happen in a certain timeframe. Isn't that the American way? Well, my friends, this spiritual pilgrimage generally doesn't work that

2. Chittister, *The Way We Were*, 181.
3. McKim, *Westminster Dictionary of Theological Terms*, 78.

way! God's timeframe isn't ours. Often we don't have the patience and courage to wait for God's timing and God's process to bring about what is best for God's kingdom versus our own agenda.

How to be Strong and Courageous

God knows that humans by nature are not patient and have trouble hoping in something that they can't see, which is often the case with discernment on this spiritual pilgrimage. But God wants to encourage us to march on. After Moses' death the Lord spoke to Joshua, and Joshua 1:1–10 has some important advice for all of us. Three times during this short passage the Lord tells Joshua to be "strong and courageous," in order for the Israelites to receive the land promised to them. They are also told to meditate on God's word day and night. This sounds to me like the spiritual practices that we have talked about. Verse nine is a good summary of this passage, "I hereby command you: Be strong and courageous; do not be frightened or dismayed, for the Lord your God is with you wherever you go." Just as the Lord was with the Israelites, God will be with us as well and will provide discernment for the next step.

Being strong and courageous is easy to talk about when everything is going along smoothly, but how about when we have pain, sorrow, or difficult times in our lives? Nowhere in the Bible that I know of does it say that our lives will be without challenges and totally perfect. However, the Lord does say in many places that God will be with us. This verse from Joshua says that God will be with us wherever we go; that means if it is in the valley, the desert, or the oasis times of our lives, God will be there.

When we meditate on God's ways day and night, we are able to be strong and courageous in what God wants for

Discernment

us. Discernment evolves from this process; it may be clear or cloudy, quick, or slow in coming, but it does come. The main aspect about discernment is that *our* vision and wisdom are limited, while *God's* is unlimited. This is a difficult but important concept regarding the spiritual pilgrimage, especially in our society where we want *instant everything*.

God's Vision and Our Vision

"The plans of the mind belong to mortals, but the answer of the tongue is from the Lord. All one's ways may be pure in one's own eyes, but the Lord weighs the spirit. Commit your work to the Lord, and your plans will be established. The human mind plans the way, but the Lord directs the steps," (Proverbs 16:1–3, 9). Throughout time humans have always thought that they were smarter, wiser, more intelligent than the Lord God or any other god. Beginning with the Enlightenment down through the time of the Industrial Revolution, and more recently throughout the past century, society has invented more new gadgets, developed labor-saving devices, experienced space travel, and created the latest high-tech gizmos that have deceived us into believing that humankind doesn't necessarily need an old-fashioned, all-knowing God any longer.

However, in Proverbs 16 and elsewhere God makes it clear that humans can make their plans, but for those on this spiritual pilgrimage, discernment and guidance will come from the Lord. It is perfectly okay for us to think about where we need to be, but as spiritual pilgrims it is important to stop and listen to the voice of God coming through prayer and the Holy Spirit, *and let that voice guide where we should be walking next.*

As humans we are all limited in vision and wisdom, but God's vision is unlimited. It is up to us who are on this spiritual pilgrimage to be open to the discernment that will be offered, even if we think that is it slow in coming or leads us to an unknown path. Often things happen to us for reasons we may not understand until years later.

Life Decisions

As disciples on this spiritual pilgrimage all decisions matter yet God's presence and grace embraces all! In my case trying to focus on doing God's will led me to make decisions that might have been different otherwise. One major choice was my decision to attend Catholic services with my family and be involved in its activities even though I didn't officially join.

Judy and I were married for twenty-eight years when she passed away. She grew up in the Roman Catholic Church, and we were married in it and reared our children in it also. For a number of years I attended worship services in that church, and always took part in the activities. I enjoyed a number of aspects about the Catholic Church, but did not believe what the church taught about Holy Communion. That was a stumbling block for me, thus, I never joined nor received communion.

After many years of going to Catholic masses with my family, I joined a Lutheran Church (ELCA) that over time lead me to Trinity Lutheran Seminary. I needed the experience with the Catholic Church to prepare me for the Lutheran worship. It would have been much more difficult to go from the Baptist Church (where I belonged for the first twenty-seven years of my life) to the Lutheran Church without the long period in the Catholic Church. Thus, the decision made some time ago about the Catholic faith has helped move me to the point where I am now. Worshiping in the Catholic Church, however, did aid my life spiritually.

Discernment

The spiritual growth that was obtained during this time was influenced by my worship and connection to the Catholic Church.

All of life's decisions are important. When we allow the Holy Spirit to comfort and guide us, the path we take may be different from one based solely upon our own intuition. We are all on a path going somewhere, even if we are trying to stay put and not change, we are in fact changing and moving. I didn't realize when I was interacting with the Catholic Church that it would influence my joining a Lutheran Church later on. I didn't have a clue that would happen. However, God apparently knew what was coming.

There are many examples of God moving people to places they didn't know existed before they got there, but their eyes were opened to a new adventure because they were willing to listen to the guidance of the Holy Spirit. The Israelite people are a good example of that. We'll look at one small passage that relates to this concept.

Discernment on the Long Road to Freedom

> The angel of God who was going before the Israelite army moved and went behind them; and the pillar of cloud moved from in front of them and took its place behind them. It came between the army of Egypt and the army of Israel. And so the cloud was there with the darkness, and it lit up the night; one did not come near the other all night. (Exodus 14:19–20)

God through Moses guided the Israelites into the Promised Land, led them, fed them, listened to their complaining, and also got angry with them from time to time. However, this passage from Exodus 14 shows how detailed

Discipleship—A Lifelong Spiritual Pilgrimage

the protection and guidance was for the Israelites. The angel of God and pillar of cloud were at one point leading them and then changed position to protect them.

On our spiritual pilgrimage the Holy Spirit can and is doing the same for us. The Holy Spirit gives us the discernment to take the next steps along this walk. Granted, the steps may not be ones that we think may be best for us, nor do they necessarily head us in a direction in which we can see the end. Foster talks about how the Spirit of Jesus is guiding us today:

> Indeed, in movements all over the world we are now beginning to see the breathing forth of the apostolic church of the Spirit. Many are having a deep and profound experience of an Emmanuel of the Spirit—God with us; a knowledge that in the power of the Spirit Jesus has come to guide his people himself; an experience of his leading that is as definite and as immediate as the cloud by day and the pillar of fire by night.[4]

This guidance is as definite and immediate as it was for Moses and the Israelites. The Holy Spirit is there to help us strive for God's kingdom, and the discernment, if followed, will help guide us in that direction, toward God's will versus our own agenda. As the Israelites were led to freedom and to a new life and land so we, too, are led to freedom—the freedom to let go of those aspects of our life that are keeping us from becoming the people that God wants us to be. This freedom empowers us to become witnesses for Jesus to the ends of the world.

This pilgrimage in the world, however, does not come with a roadmap. Martha Stortz writes, "We have no maps for the journey of discipleship. . . . But disciples follow a person, and to move forward, we need to listen for his

4. Foster, *Celebration*, 175.

voice."[5] When we pray, and listen to this voice direction and discernment will come; however, it may not come in a manner or custom in which we are used to receiving. It's highly unlikely that our travels will take us on a well-lighted six-lane super highway with the latest GPS available for our use! Our guidance comes from the Holy Spirit who directs us as God's angel guided the Israelites and as Jesus gave direction to his followers. All of this is possible for those who are serious travelers on this spiritual pilgrimage.

Loving God and Called to God's Purpose

The passage from Romans 8:28, in some scholars' minds, is quoted for the wrong reasons when talking about discernment. "We know that all things work together for good for those who love God, who are called according to his purpose." Most people quote the first part about "all things working together for good" to show that God wants everyone to have some kind of perfect life. The rest of the verse is the actual key, however: if we love God and are called to God's purpose, all things will work together when God's love and will are leading us versus following our own agenda. The purpose of this guidance and discernment are not, however, to neatly tie together our life like a gift with a big fancy bow. Rather, it is to have us turn toward the love of God and strive for God's kingdom. God's purpose for us comes from God's will not ours.

Discernment—Round and Round

There is a verse in a child's song, "The wheels on the bus go round and round, round and round." In the same way the

5. Stortz, *Blessed to Follow*, 33.

discernment process also goes round and round. Following discernment, some action may happen immediately or a period of waiting may ensue; but in either case the cycle happens over and over again as long as we continue on our spiritual pilgrimage. Each day brings with it a new set of lenses, a new step, and a new view of this pilgrimage. Our role is to daily continue striving for God's kingdom to become a more faithful disciple. Discernment will come out of this through the Holy Spirit, while we are on this earthly walk.

This centuries-old prayer for discernment has helped me in my pilgrimage. May you find guidance and hope in it as well: "I believe I am always divinely guided. I believe I will always take the right turn of the road. I believe God will always make a way where there is no way."

Questions for Discussion

1. We pray, "God's will be done." How do you discern God's will in your daily life?

2. What does the word "discernment" mean to you? Have you ever been given direct or indirect discernment? Did you follow through with taking the steps? If not, talk about the barriers or roadblocks.

3. When was a time in your past when you received discernment and it changed or redirected your life?

4. What new adventure do you think God is calling you to do in your life right now?

Discernment

For Additional Reflection

- Ponder the times in your life when you had to make decisions that you knew would cause controversy for your family or friends. Record a couple of these in your journal.
- Be open to letting go of your limited vision, giving way to God's unlimited vision.
- Reflect on 1 Kings 3 about how Solomon asked God for a discerning and understanding mind.

SIX

Hope

Hope and faith are inextricably linked: If I believe in God the Creator, then I must hope in this God's commitment to the eternally ongoing process of Creation. I am not born finished.[1]

—JOAN CHITTISTER

Hope in God's Ongoing Process of Creation

To follow the discernment we will be given on this spiritual pilgrimage, we have to have hope in the promises of God. It doesn't matter that during our spiritual practices the Holy Spirit reveals a next step if we aren't willing to take it. We all have moments in our lives when we doubt a proposed action or are afraid to choose between several paths.

At some point during this process we will be called upon to step out in faith not knowing how things may turn out, only that it appears we are being led to do so. We have been talking all along that this pilgrimage is a process

1. Chittister, *In Search*, 150.

Hope

without an ending. There isn't some mythical finish line that will be crossed on this side of the kingdom. It is important during this process to have hope, not in the process of this spiritual pilgrimage, nor in our spiritual practices, but hope in the One into whom these activities bring us into a closer relationship—God the Creator. Our hope as fallible human beings is that God has made a commitment to this ongoing process of creation, accompanying us on this pathway throughout our lives and into the life to come.

As we strive first for the kingdom of God, while engaging in spiritual practices and becoming the person that God wants us to be, our hope is in God the Creator. Having this hope is essential so that we don't become discouraged and attempt to find another way to live.

God's Hope Different than Wishful Thinking

> Hope is trusting that something will be fulfilled, but fulfilled according to the promises and not just according to our wishes. Therefore, hope is always open-ended. I have found it very important in my own life to let go of my wishes and start hoping. It was only when I was willing to let go of wishes that something really new, something beyond my own expectations, could happen to me.[2]

When I was younger, I read a lot of positive thinking books, which at the time did offer me help as I was trying to find out who I was meant to be. However, my view of how my spiritual pilgrimage shapes up today is that I can't project a future happening unless it is fashioned around the promised hope of God. As a human with an active imagination I

2. Nouwen, *Seeds of Hope*, 159–60.

am always getting carried away with all sorts of ideas about my future and the future of my family, friends, and how the world should be. But more and more of my wishful thinking has given way to hoping in the promises of God, which opens all of us up for things that could have never been dreamed about otherwise.

"For in hope we were saved. Now hope that is seen is not hope. For who hopes for what is seen? But if we hope for what we do not see, we wait for it with patience" (Romans 8:24–25). On this spiritual pilgrimage we should strive to be open-minded, letting go of our wishes, having patience as we put our hope in God's promises, and allowing this hope to take us to places we may never have thought about before. We may not be able to see these new places, but God knows that they are there. These new places will be filled with all of the aspects of this world that will include joy as well as suffering.

Hope Despite Suffering

> Therefore, since we are justified by faith, we have peace with God through our Lord Jesus Christ, through whom we have obtained access to this grace in which we stand; and we boast in our hope of sharing the glory of God. And not only that, but we also boast in our sufferings, knowing that suffering produces endurance, and endurance produces character, and character produces hope, and hope does not disappoint us, because God's love has been poured into our hearts through the Holy Spirit that has been given to us. (Romans 5:1–5)

Our daily life experiences, especially our times of suffering, can offer us some insight into this spiritual pilgrimage. Paul,

Hope

in his letter to the Romans, writes that suffering produces endurance, which produces character, which produces hope. Of course, none of us should seek out suffering, however, sometimes it can't be avoided.

Let's consider for a moment that suffering plus God equals hope! Paul asserts that suffering is a first step on the pilgrimage to sharing God's glory. Paul knows that humans often interpret suffering as something to be avoided at all costs, but suffering can lead to God's glory and hope. If we are trying to persevere through the sufferings by our own efforts, or trying to think our way through, or trying to wait it out, or trying to dismiss or quickly forget what caused the suffering, we may ignore the peace and love of God in our midst, and we may also not come to realize the hope that God wants us to have.

Paul writes to the Romans to remind them that they have the peace of God through Jesus Christ, and that the Holy Spirit is giving them God's love. He wanted them to think on these things when they were suffering. The same is true for us today.

Hope for the Present Moment

When we are going through a time of suffering, trying to keep the faith can be a very difficult thing to do. Many of our family members and friends may be telling us daily to just take it one day at a time, relax, and things will work out. However, we are the ones going through the challenges and dealing with things that can turn out to be quite an ordeal. Nouwen gives us some good food for thought about the hope for the present moment. "Hope frees us from the need to predict the future and allows us to live in the present, with the deep trust that God will never leave us alone but will fulfill the deepest desires of our heart."[3] When we are able to step back and objectively look at a negative situation we can see how having hope in God or something greater than ourselves does help us out. Additionally, when we step back and look at what God has done for us in the past, we can give up trying to predict the future and live in the present moment. Our hope can come from that deep trust that God will never leave us alone.

However, there are those times in our lives when what we are going through is so drastic and severe that our rational mind and spirit can begin to feel trapped, as in quicksand preventing our bodies from moving anywhere. Sometimes all of the supportive comments and positive feedback from those around us just bounce off us and don't sink in because of the awful position we are in at the moment. The love and hope of God are there, but we aren't able to experience it as we'd like.

Taking it one day at a time and living in the moment sounds fine, but our body and mind aren't always able to deal with that concept because all of our physical and emotional energy is consumed with trying to untangle ourselves from that which has encircled us. Having God's hope in our heart sounds fine but sometimes it just doesn't make logical sense to us.

Judy's Cancer

Sometimes holding onto hope can be difficult regardless of how strong our prayer life is or how long we have been on our spiritual pilgrimage. A couple of times in this book I have mentioned the situation with my late wife's battle with brain tumors. When I was dealing with her cancer and the

---

3. Nouwen, *Here and Now*, 41.

related side effects of it, I tried to live in the present moment, during that time. God's love and presence became real to me in ways that I couldn't have envisioned until I hit bottom. "Even though I walk through the darkest valley, I fear no evil; your rod and your staff—they comfort me," (Psalm 23:4).

Judy's second operation to remove the brain tumor and the period of recovery that followed was a growing time for me and one that definitely changed me. Yes, many times during that period I felt that I was in the darkest valley. Having hope in God and taking it one day at a time took on a new and powerful meaning for me. Judy spent twelve weeks in two hospitals and a nursing home learning to talk, walk, speak, and somewhat take care of her personal needs. From that time on she did not work or drive again. Someone had to be with her at night, and my life changed in so many ways that it's impossible to list all of them. Over time she came to have a moderate quality of life until the tumor came back yet again.

Judy's Last Seven Months

Devastatingly in the spring of 1998 some of the dreaded symptoms reappeared. After all of the tests and consultation with the specialists, it was determined that her tumor was back. But this time our options were limited. She'd already had two surgeries and a third one was not feasible. Chemotherapy would only slow the tumor's growth and cause undesirable side effects. She had already been given radiation, and it couldn't be repeated. After many discussions and prayers we decided to make her comfortable for her remaining days, which the doctors believed would be about six months.

Discipleship—A Lifelong Spiritual Pilgrimage

Hospice became involved because I wanted to keep her at home. *But, I didn't fully know what I was getting into!* As the tumor grew it slowly took away her ability to take care of herself. As that happened, we had to do more for her. A hospice aid came in three mornings a week to give her a bed bath. The rest of the mornings, the evenings, and weekends were my responsibility to care for her. After a while I looked into a few private-care firms but they didn't work out. However, my employer allowed me to work out of my home so I could care for her since someone had to be with her at all times.

I am one of those people who dislike hospitals and nursing homes and always had a hard time being around them. So for me to have a hospital bed in our dining room and to have to do some of the things I had to do took a lot of my physical and emotional energy. Without going into graphic details I will only say that the tumor slowly took away Judy's ability to care for herself. For three months I did most of the physical care of Judy by myself, and also tried to keep things going with my job to the fullest of my ability. People offered to help and friends and people from our churches provided meals.

Both of our extended families were nearly four hours away. They supported us with prayers, cards, and phone calls. My mom was able to visit a couple of times and assisted us. Judy's parents had already passed away. My son, Kevin, who was twenty-three at the time, was in college. He came home to stay with us and was a huge help. My daughter, Elizabeth, lived close by but was kept busy with her very young daughter.

Hope

Hitting the Brick Wall

One Wednesday, after three months of providing constant care to Judy, I hit a brick wall and couldn't do anymore. I was mentally, physically, and emotionally exhausted and lost nearly all hope that I could go on any longer. I had never felt like this before. Every day I struggled just to get up in the morning. Judy and I had always worked together to handle life's situations. But we never had faced a challenge like this one. I am one of those hardheaded people who hate asking for help, but I was at the end of my resources at this point.

I called my associate pastor and the parish nurse. They came over immediately to provide support. The parish nurse had offered help before. (She together with other women from the churches, and a hospice volunteer would stay with Judy whenever I had to go out.) I finally admitted that I couldn't handle it alone any longer.

To make a long story short, after some organization, the parish nurse enlisted women from the health and wellness committee to come over and help with Judy in the evenings when I needed it most. We were also able to get help from some women from Judy's church as well. Additionally, a neighbor and a friend helped out.

God's Help in the Form of Angels

From Psalm 91:11–12 we have a great passage about angels helping us. "For he will command his angels concerning you to guard you in all your ways. On their hands they will bear you up, so that you will not dash your foot against a stone." Those wonderful women who came and helped out were like angels to me, because they also talked with and listened to me. Since I worked at home, I did not always have a lot of human interaction during the day. Over time Judy lost her ability to talk. So, their visits helped me in two ways: their care of Judy as well as conversation for me. Those times of fellowship were one of the reasons I made it through this period. I also had to face the fact that I was losing my wife and best friend of more than twenty-eight years. Depression, fatigue, and hopelessness were all present during that time. Those women shared my emotional burden and helped me make it through each day. They supported me through the toughest thing I have ever had to do in my life. They helped me in those *final months* until Judy died.

I experienced so many emotions and feelings at that time. My pain and stress during those months were unimaginable. The women who helped me were God's vessels of love and hope reaching out to me. No one can ever tell me that the Holy Spirit was not in Judy's room during the seven months and especially on the night that she died. The Spirit was there in the love from the people who helped us and the love that I gave in taking care of her as she would have done for me. During this long and painful process, how I viewed God's love, and what God had for me to do on this side of the kingdom became clearer to me.

My prayer continued to be, "Help me to be able to contend with just one day at a time, Lord; also, help Judy to go peacefully and without pain." She passed away on January 23, 1999 and we were able to keep her at home the entire time, through prayer and God's grace, hope, and love given in so many ways. From what we could tell she never had any pain from the tumor, and she did die peacefully.

Hope

God's Hope in the Pain and Suffering

The grieving period after she died was terribly painful. I prayed to God that the pain would go away, but it didn't. I kept on praying because that was all I could do. As human beings we don't want to suffer nor have a God that suffers. Often our God is a projection made in our own image. We want glory, not suffering. However, God suffers with us and walks with us through the pain. Douglas John Hall wrote; "Christian hope . . . is hope in a God who loves the world, [and] who is determined to redeem it."[4] God is a God who loves the world so much and redeemed it through Jesus Christ, God's only begotten son who suffers with us. Our Christian hope grows out of God's love for us and the world.

We see the effect of this growth when we go through times of suffering. The struggle is a necessary part of our Christian growth and spiritual pilgrimage. Our faith and hope grow as we go through life; it's all a process. Again Paul in Romans 5 reminds us that suffering produces endurance, which produces character, which produces hope, and hope does not disappoint us. The hope obtained during this process is a precious gift on our pilgrimage.

Throughout Judy's illness and during my grief after her death, I, somehow, had to keep on going; I couldn't stop and totally give up. I was called to move on. The only hope I had was that God was in the grieving and pain with me. "And now, O Lord, what do I wait for? My hope is in you" (Psalm 39:7). God's presence helped me to get through to the other side of the pain to a new tomorrow. God doesn't make bad things happen; however, God works through the bad things to bring something better for God's kingdom.

As humans we cry out to God in our weakness and suffering. Sometimes we bring suffering on ourselves when we

---

4. Hall, *Confessing the Faith*, 497.

pull away from God. Suffering is at times a consequence of our thoughts, deeds, and actions. Of course, hurtful things can also happen to us that are outside of our control. Events such as floods, earthquakes, brain tumors, and disease can come upon us. We can also suffer when our sin pulls us from God's purpose and direction. However, because of the love that God has for humankind, God suffers right along with us in whatever happens in our lives, whether it is natural evil, or things caused by our own actions. When I focus on the kingdom of God, my anxiety is greatly reduced. My focus is not on me but rather on what God wants me to do in this life for God's kingdom.

Hope in this Spiritual Pilgrimage

As you can tell from my story, no matter how much we want to become a more faithful disciple and walk the path of this spiritual pilgrimage we can't avoid tragedy and pain along the way. By embarking on a spiritual pilgrimage or enhancing it, God's love and hope will become more apparent in our daily walk, giving us the courage to go on. The hope and love are always there, though sometimes it is hard to see. In my case I had to hit rock bottom before being willing to fully embrace it. God's hope leads us to the next step of this pilgrimage, a faith that equals trust.

Questions for Discussion

1. Do you agree with the statement, *God's hope is different from wishful thinking*? Explain.
2. Have you ever had a time in your life when you were suffering and couldn't feel God's love and hope? Did

you believe that it would ever come? How did you get through it?

3. Have you ever been the bearer of God's hope in a painful situation? Reflect upon that experience.

For Additional Reflection

- Read stories about other people's life challenges where God's hope was revealed.
- Pick out examples of hope from the Bible (the Psalms and Proverbs are a good place to start). Use them as part of your daily devotions, and consider focusing on a short passage over a period of time to let the words soak in.

SEVEN

Faith Equals Trust

Faith is a relational concept. It is another word for trust, and its application to God (faith *in* God) is in essence not different from its application to other relationships. . . . Like these relationships, faith in God is always a matter of decision and is not a fixed quality but a response that demands continuous renewal.[1]

—DOUGLAS JOHN HALL

We've talked about how it was important to hope in God throughout our spiritual pilgrimage and how at times this hope can be difficult to envision. It is vital, however, that we continue moving forward with hope during the times of spiritual darkness until the light once again better illuminates our path. Hope in God, poured out on us through the Holy Spirit, strengthens our faith and carries us forward, to a point in which we can more fully trust in God's promises.

One of the constant themes of this pilgrimage is that it is a continuous process, not a fixed quality, but a continuous change and renewal. This change comes about because

1. Hall, *Bound and Free*, 116.

of the function of the Holy Spirit and the ongoing renewal occurring within us. Each day of this pilgrimage brings something new. Lamentations 3:22–23a tells us that "The steadfast love of the Lord never ceases, his mercies never come to an end; they are new every morning." God's mercies are *new* every morning, and every day the Holy Spirit gives new insight into God's grace, love, and hope, thus, changing how we view and live our life.

Faith is Trust in God

Faith and trust are synonymous. If faith is trust in God, then the disciple must trust that God is in the future as well as the present. Therefore, the disciple can walk into the future even when the future is full of doubt and uncertainty. 1 Peter 1:21 tells us "Through him [Jesus] you have come to trust in God, who raised him from the dead and gave him glory, so that your faith and hope are set on God." A helpful explanation of this verse from the Lutheran Study Bible note states: "The saving gift that Christ brings is trust in God. This trust defines the faith of God's people." Faith and trust are used interchangeably, but they both point to having hope in God through Jesus Christ. This chapter will delve into this aspect of the spiritual walk.

The Meaning of Faith

> Now faith is the assurance of things hoped for, the conviction of things not seen. Indeed, by faith our ancestors received approval. By faith we understand that the worlds were prepared by the word of God, so that what is seen was made from things that are not visible. . . . And without

> faith it is impossible to please God, for whoever would approach him must believe that he exists and that he rewards those who seek him. (Hebrews 11:1–3, 6)

Faith is what we hope for but can't see. Most of us are familiar with this passage that gives examples of those who have gone before us and showed great faith in their own individual walk. Most of the passages begin with "by faith." It is by faith that these trusting people stepped out not knowing the exact outcome or result beforehand, but their faith in God allowed them to believe and act on the promises made.

By faith Abel offered God a greater sacrifice than Cain's, by faith Abraham obeyed, and by faith Moses' parents hid him, etc. They didn't just sit on their hands and cry, *woe is me*, nor did they tell God *no*, when God asked them to move forward. Their faith grew out of their relationship with God and allowed them to do something! Their faith propelled them into action.

Faith Implies Action

Faith implies action! If we believe that something may happen, we'll put ourselves into a position to help make that happen. On the other hand, if we are doubtful that something can happen, or we can't see it with our limited vision, then we are inclined to do nothing. Thus, if we are in a drought and we pray for rain, do we have our umbrella out? If praying for healing, do we do all we can to assist the healing? If we want to experience spiritual growth as an individual, do we invest time and effort into our prayer lives and other spiritual disciplines?

Are we willing to pray, listen, discern, and then take steps based on the guidance of the Holy Spirit as we walk

Faith Equals Trust

along our spiritual pilgrimage? Are we willing to believe and have faith that Jesus can still perform miracles in our lives when we are striving first for the kingdom of God and seeking to do God's will in our everyday lives? Are we willing to risk change in our lives in becoming the person God wants us to be? Are we willing to be open to the joy and blessings that can be ours?

Answered Prayer

All of these may be good questions and cause us to reflect deeply upon our faith in God. In Mark 11:20–25 Jesus taught about praying without doubting, and believing that what you ask for will be given. Sometimes God does directly answer our prayers. Let me share an example of that from my early days.

In my youth I was a member of Jerusalem Baptist Church, in Youngstown, Ohio and had been very involved with the church. I began to feel the love of God as I got older and started to trust the love and direction that were given. A defining point for me was when I was in my high school locker room after gym one day, maybe in the tenth grade. Guys often made fun of me when I changed clothes because of being overweight. One day I prayed that God would stop them from talking about me, and they did! This was the first time I knew God directly answered my prayer. One minute they were making fun and the next minute they were not. I was still overweight and they could make fun of me again, but at that moment I knew God was there and cared about me. I had attended church and Sunday school since I could remember, and had learned all of the Bible stories, but this moment brought all that experience and education into focus. Needless to say, prayer doesn't always work that way, but it did for me at that moment.

Discipleship—A Lifelong Spiritual Pilgrimage

Looking again at Mark 11:23–24, the note on this passage from the Lutheran Study Bible offers good insight into this passage. "The point is not that if you pray for something and it does not happen, you did not have enough faith. Rather, when you have faith, your prayers tend to line up with those things that God wants to happen (see 1 Cor 13:2). God wants us to pray, hears our prayers, and responds to them."

When we are on this spiritual pilgrimage, striving for God's kingdom and become engaged with or enhancing our spiritual practices, we will become more of the person God created us to be, and thus able to see life with a new and different lens. When our faith is in God, our actions keep us better focused on the things of the kingdom, versus our own agenda. Our prayers and expectations become aligned with God's will.

Unanswered Prayers

Sometimes God does answer our prayer in one form or the other. However, I can't begin to count the number of times that I have fervently prayed for some outcome and it didn't turn out the way I wanted. You can probably say the same thing. That doesn't mean, however, that God doesn't love us or isn't concerned about our daily needs. God is love and can't help but love us, but God isn't required to answer every request we make.

God wants us to keep on praying as we walk on this pilgrimage because it draws us closer to God. Faith implies action and our action is to keep on keeping on. There will be times of doubt along the way and we can't get around that. Douglas John Hall wrote, "A faith that does not doubt is a dead faith."[2] If we never doubted God, our faith could

---

2. Hall, *Bound and Free*, 117.

Faith Equals Trust

be dead or dying. Never doubting could mean that we are not fully engaging ourselves in our life, because as we live and function situations will cause us to doubt at times.

As finite humans on this side of the kingdom in all its fullness, we will have doubts, fears, and concerns no matter how long we have been on this pilgrimage. But God wants us to see and walk by faith. Catherine of Genoa wrote, "But God, who desires that we see by faith and who desires that we not do good because of selfish motives, gives us this vision little by little, sufficient to the level of faith of which we are capable."[3] Having doubt is not wrong or necessarily bad, but focusing on our own selfish agenda and not being open to where God is trying to take us is certainly a concern. We must trust that God's mercies are new every morning, and cling to that promise even when we have moments of doubt.

The Meaning of Trust

Henri Nouwen once spent time in Europe with a family of trapeze artists. He noticed that as the trapeze artists threw themselves into the air, it was the catcher who did all the work in catching them. If the trapeze artist failed to trust and instead tried to grab hold of the catcher she or he might fall. The artist being caught must trust that the catcher will be successful. He felt that trusting God worked in that same way. Nouwen wrote, "In the spiritual journey, we must throw ourselves toward God and then trust that God will catch us. If, out of anxiety, we try to catch God or to control how God should catch us, we may fall."[4]

---

3. Catherine of Genoa, "Life and Teaching," 214.
4. Nouwen, *Henri Nouwen*, lix–lx.

Discipleship—A Lifelong Spiritual Pilgrimage

On our daily spiritual pilgrimage through life we have to also throw ourselves toward God and trust that, just like the catcher of the trapeze artist, God will catch us as well. Having the faith to totally trust in God may come slowly to those of us who are adults. Most children who have a loving family environment and are nourished and cared for usually have such trust in their parents. However, as the saying goes, life happens, and as we grow older we see that our parents are just as fallible as we are. We also encounter people in our daily dealings who cause us to lose our faith or trust in humankind. During such times, we may also lose our trust in God. This is especially so if we have been wronged by a church leader or religious institution of some kind.

Relearning to Trust

Learning to really trust again only comes over a long period of time in which the emotions, thoughts, and feelings of the past are healed. Taking part in these spiritual practices and being on this pilgrimage can help rebuild our broken trust. This is one way to overcome patterns of the past, but it isn't the only way. In this process of striving for God's kingdom we become a lifelong disciple.

Trust in God

There are many Scriptures revolving around trusting in God, but one of my favorites is from Psalm 37. The Psalm speaks about trusting in the Lord, taking delight in the Lord, committing to the Lord, and waiting for the Lord. Verse five is very powerful, "Commit your way to the Lord; trust in him, and he will act." As this passage states, the Lord will act in our lives when we commit our way and trust in the

Faith Equals Trust

Lord. As we read about the trapeze artist having to trust the catcher, we must trust in God and not in our own efforts.

The chapter heading in the NRSV Bible for Psalm 37 reads "Exhortation to Patience and Trust." It takes patience and trust in order to see the Lord acting in our lives. We have talked before that this pilgrimage is a process and requires us to patiently trust in God's timing and vision and not our own. When we hope in God, our trust in God increases.

If you are having a hard time trusting God because of certain things you are going through at this time, may this centuries-old prayer give you some comfort: "Let nothing disturb you, let nothing frighten you, all things will pass away except God; God alone is sufficient," (adapted from St. Teresa of Avila).

Faith and Trust on this Spiritual Pilgrimage

Nouwen gives us more insightful thoughts to help us along this way: "Faith is the deep trust that God's love is stronger than all the anonymous powers of the world and can transform us from victims of darkness into servants of light."[5] What a powerful statement for those who have been beaten down by life, or may be going through a dark period. We need to hear over and over again that faith is the deep trust that God's love is stronger than anything else.

This understanding that faith is trust in God's love can indeed change us and take us to new and exciting places that we never thought of before. On this spiritual pilgrimage it is vital to be open to how the Holy Spirit may be changing us and where the Spirit may be taking us. Like the

---

5. Nouwen, *Here and Now*, 105.

trapeze artist, we will throw ourselves out there and trust in the catcher, who is God.

Our spiritual pilgrimage is a process of hope and of trusting in God's promises that God will always be with us. This is all about becoming a more faithful disciple. In the last chapter of this book we will take a closer look at what the concept of discipleship means.

Questions for Discussion

1. What does this statement mean to you: "Faith is trust in God"?

2. Who are some of the role models in your life who helped you learn about trusting in God? What did they do?

3. What challenging task has God called you to do? How have you responded?

4. How is having faith connected to taking some action?

For Additional Reflection

- There are many Scriptures on faith. Read and reflect on them. Start with the books of Matthew, Romans, and also Hebrews 11.

- Many of the Psalms and especially Psalm 37 are good ones to reflect on about trusting in God.

- Faith implies action. Reflect on times in your life where your pilgrimage caused you to step out in faith to take actions that you didn't think were possible. Record a few in your journal.

EIGHT

Discipleship

The word *disciple* occurs 269 times in the New Testament. *Christian* is found only three times and was first introduced to refer precisely to the disciples. . . . The New Testament is a book about disciples, by disciples, and for disciples of Jesus Christ. . . . The disciple of Christ desires above all else to be like him.[1]

—DALLAS WILLARD

IN MATTHEW 28 JESUS commissions the disciples after his resurrection. He tells them to go and make disciples of all nations. Note that Jesus didn't say to establish large institutions or start religious organizations. Humankind started those as the movement progressed. However, the message from Jesus was fairly simple: go and make disciples. The word "disciple" is used often in the New Testament to refer to those who followed Jesus. As we have talked about this spiritual pilgrimage, we keep going back to the concept of becoming a more faithful disciple and the person that God wants us to be.

---

1. Willard, "The Spirit of the Disciplines," 14–15.

Discipleship—A Lifelong Spiritual Pilgrimage

Discipleship Means Always Learning

In his last part of the commissioning of the disciples, Jesus tells his disciples to teach those nations all that Jesus had taught them. In Matthew 28:20a he said "And teaching them to obey everything that I have commanded you." Besides making disciples of all nations and baptizing them, they were also to teach them.

The word "disciple" means above all else—*learner* or *pupil*. We will always be learning about God's kingdom and our call/role in that kingdom. Striving for God's kingdom and being a disciple on this spiritual pilgrimage is a lifelong learning process. It is one that is never finished on this side of the kingdom in its fullness.

Jesus Freed Us to Become More Faithful Disciples

Jesus is about teaching and freeing people in a way that had never been done before. This freedom comes about because of what people learn from his teaching as well as through his sacrifice of love. We were freed to become the persons that God created us to be, to live as faithful disciples. We gain freedom and knowledge as God's people through conversion, spiritual practices, and striving for God's kingdom. Foster talks about how freedom is a by-product of discipline and commitment.

> Demosthenes was free to be a great orator only because he had gone through the discipline of speaking above the roar of the ocean with pebbles in his mouth. George Frederick Handel was able to compose his magnificent Messiah only because he had schooled himself in musical composition. By means of intense personal discipline Flannery O'Connor was able to rise

above a debilitating disease to become one of the finest fiction writers of the twentieth century. Freedom is the product of discipline and commitment.[2]

Discipline and commitment are needed to become a lifelong learning disciple. As already stated this process requires time spent in reading, studying, reflecting, and absorbing the word of God into our very being. It means letting the word grow and mature in our hearts and souls as we walk the spiritual pilgrimage to which God has called us. Without the discipline and commitment of daily spiritual practices we aren't as able to open our heart, soul, and mind to learn about and see God's vision for us. It is important to remain and continue in the word of God, to have the word live in us, which leads to freedom. This freedom then allows us to walk where God calls us.

Our Freedom is Not for Us Alone

Dwelling in the truth of Jesus, we are free to be that person who is able to live into a life unencumbered by the things that hold us back from becoming the person God wants us to be. We are free to become more faithful disciples on this pilgrimage knowing that no matter what happens in this life or in the one to come we are loved by God, whose essence is love, and who can't stop loving us no matter what happens. God's *truth* through the word makes us free. On our spiritual pilgrimage we need to continue in the word of Jesus and look for the Holy Spirit to guide our way, and then we are free to live without the worries of the world that would enslave us.

---

2. Foster, *Prayer*, 67–68.

Discipleship—A Lifelong Spiritual Pilgrimage

Free to Witness

Being freed by Jesus carries with it a responsibility to be open to witnessing to others about the awesome love of God in our lives. In Mark 6:6b–13, Jesus sends his disciples out to proclaim the message of repentance, to cast out demons, and heal the sick. As disciples today we have an obligation to reach out to those who are enslaved by doubts and fears and don't know of the love of God that can free them.

Being set free means having our desires and centeredness turned from us toward God and others. *The purpose of growing as disciples is for the sake of God's entire creation, for making disciples, for loving, and for healing our broken world.* We keep our eyes on the cross, on Jesus, so that we become bolder disciples and witnesses.

Discipleship is being a Disciple of Jesus Christ

"Discipleship is not a program, a life style, an agenda. Christians are disciples of *Jesus Christ*. . . . Discipleship as worldly responsibility means obedience to the living Lord in the midst of a living, changing world; the ethic that belongs to this life is a thoroughly contextual ethic."[3] Discipleship is totally about being a disciple of *Jesus Christ*—that needs to be understood very clearly. This doesn't involve worshiping a person in our culture nor following a movement apart from Christianity. When any person or organization attempts to direct you toward another path, pray that the Holy Spirit will guide you back to striving for God's kingdom and becoming a witness to Jesus.

In Matthew 5:1, which begins the Sermon on the Mount, Jesus teaches his *followers* so many things, but his teaching wasn't meant for everyone. "When Jesus saw the

3. Hall, *Confessing the Faith*, 336.

Discipleship

crowds, he went up the mountain; and after he sat down, his disciples came to him. Then he began to speak and taught them." Jesus taught his disciples in this passage and not necessarily the mass of people who followed him. Thus, the Sermon on the Mount was for his closest followers and not in this case for those who were unwilling or unable to commit to the discipline of following Jesus.

What Happens Now?

At this point a person reading this could say, well, what does this mean to me? From my viewpoint, by continuing to strive for God's kingdom today, I know that God will reveal more and more of the vision that God has for me. As God opens my heart and mind to God's will and I am open to more of God's love, my understanding of God will change and evolve one day at a time. My life's view and the world around me will change during my spiritual pilgrimage, as the practices of prayer, Bible study, and reflection deepen and grow.

As humans we can never in our present state know all there is to know about God. However, I've realized that learning about God is a lifelong process that happens each day of our lives. The Holy Spirit is daily moving me to the place where my talents can be best used for the kingdom of God here and now. The Holy Spirit will do the same for all those who are open to the Spirit's direction. Our pilgrimage *is* a process and never finished until we see God face to face.

God's Kingdom

Jesus Christ brought the kingdom of God when he came. In Mark 1:15 he says it clearly, "The time is fulfilled, and the kingdom of God has come near; repent, and believe in the good news." God's voice through the gospel shows us how to be a part of God's kingdom that is already here. We are actively participating in the kingdom of God on earth when we strive to do God's will. The gospel is the living voice of the loving God who wants to be in a relationship with all of humankind. The word of God within the gospel is what we listen to while striving for God's kingdom.

May God's love and grace uphold and fill your life through the Holy Spirit as you grow in your spiritual pilgrimage, always striving for God's kingdom. May being a lifelong learning disciple mean for you the freedom to be Jesus' witness and to love and teach those to whom God sends you!

Questions for Discussion

1. In your daily pilgrimage, where do you struggle most to remain committed to this path? How can this be changed over time?

2. Before you read this chapter what was your concept of the word "disciple"? How has it changed?

3. What guiding principles and values in your life have you taken for granted, but now might need to change?

4. How has your life as a disciple impacted those around you?

For Additional Reflection

- Regular community worship helps one stay focused on this path. Commit to regular attendance in public worship.

Discipleship

- Think of joining a small group to pray with you, to study the Bible with you, to reflect together with you on spiritual readings. This will also help you stay on your path of discipleship.
- Becoming a disciple gives one the freedom to witness about God's love. How can you best witness to this love in your daily walk in a loving manner? Come up with a few concrete ways of doing this.
- Being a disciple above all else means learner and pupil. This pilgrimage is an ongoing process of learning how to become a disciple. Think of areas of your life that you may need additional learning. List them and begin to address them in the future.
- Discipleship is about discipline and commitment. Think about what you can give up or start doing to allow this to happen.

BIBLIOGRAPHY

Bass, Diana Butler. *Christianity for the Rest of Us: How the Neighborhood Church is Transforming the Faith.* New York: HarperCollins, 2006.

Bondi, Roberta C. *A Place to Pray: Reflections on the Lord's Prayer.* Nashville: Abingdon, 1998.

Catherine of Genoa. "Life and Teachings." In *Devotional Classics,* edited by Richard J. Foster and James Bryan Smith, 214. New York: HarperCollins, 1993.

Chittister, Joan D. *In Search of Belief.* Liguori, MO: Liguori/Triumph, 2006.

———. *The Way We Were: A Story of Conversion and Renewal.* Maryknoll, NY: Orbis, 2005.

———. *Wisdom Distilled from the Daily: Living the Rule of St. Benedict Today.* New York: HarperCollins, 1990.

Foster, Richard J. *Celebration of Discipline: The Path to Spiritual Growth.* New York: HarperCollins, 1998.

———. *Prayer: Finding the Heart's True Home.* New York: HarperCollins, 1992.

Hall, Douglas John. *Bound and Free: A Theologian's Journey.* Minneapolis: Fortress, 2005.

———. *Confessing The Faith: Christian Theology in a North American Context.* Minneapolis: Fortress, 1996.

Jones, E. Stanley. "Conversion." In *Devotional Classics,* edited by Richard J. Foster and James Bryan Smith, 303. New York: HarperCollins, 1993.

Ladd, George Eldon, and Donald Alfred Hagner. *A Theology of the New Testament.* Grand Rapids: Eerdmans, 1993.

Luther, Martin. "The Small Catechism." In *The Book of Concord: The Confessions of the Evangelical Lutheran Church*, edited by Robert Kolb and Timothy J. Wengert, 359. Minneapolis: Fortress, 2000.

Bibliography

McKim, Donald K. *Westminster Dictionary of Theological Terms.* Louisville: Westminster John Knox, 1996.

Merton, Thomas. *Contemplative Prayer.* Reprint. New York: Image, 1969.

Minor, Mitzi L. *The Power of Mark's Story.* St. Louis: Chalice, 2001.

Nouwen, Henri J. M. *Henri Nouwen: Writings Selected With an Introduction by Robert A. Jonas.* Maryknoll, NY: Orbis, 1998.

———. *Here and Now: Living in the Spirit.* New York: Crossroad, 1994.

———. *Out of Solitude: Three Meditations on the Christian Life.* Notre Dame, IN: Ave Maria, 2004.

———. *Seeds of Hope: A Henri Nouwen Reader.* Edited by Robert Durback. Reprint. New York: Image, 1997.

Tunseth, Scout, et al. *Lutheran Study Bible: New Revised Standard Version.* Minneapolis: Fortress, 2009.

Stortz, Martha E. *Blessed to Follow: The Beatitudes as a Compass for Discipleship.* Minneapolis: Augsburg Fortress, 2008.

Willard, Dallas. "The Spirit of the Disciplines." In *Devotional Classics*, edited by Richard J. Foster and James Bryan Smith, 14–15. New York: HarperCollins, 1993.

FOR ADDITIONAL READING

Bass, Diana Butler. *Strength for the Journey: A Pilgrimage of Faith in Community*. San Francisco: Jossey-Bass, 2002.

Bondi, Roberta C. *A Place To Pray: Reflections on the Lord's Prayer*. Nashville: Abingdon, 1998.

———. *To Pray and to Love: Conversations on Prayer with the Early Church*. Minneapolis: Fortress, 1991.

Bonhoeffer, Dietrich. *The Cost of Discipleship*. New York: Touchstone, 1995.

———. *Life Together: The Classic Exploration of Christian Community*. New York: HarperCollins, 1954.

Book of Common Worship, Daily Prayer. Louisville: Westminster John Knox, 1993.

Chittister, Joan D. *The Breath of the Soul: Reflections on Prayer*. New London, CT: Twenty-Third, 2010.

———. *Illuminated Life: Monastic Wisdom for Seekers of Light*. Maryknoll, NY: Orbis, 2000.

———. *In Search of Belief*. Liguori, MO: Liguori/Triumph, 2006.

———. *Wisdom Distilled from the Daily: Living the Rule of St. Benedict Today*. New York: HarperCollins, 1990.

Christensen, Bernhard. *The Inward Pilgrimage: An Introduction to Christian Spiritual Classics*. Minneapolis: Fortress, 1996.

Devotional Classics: Selected Readings for Individuals and Groups. Edited by Richard J. Foster and James Bryan Smith. New York: HarperCollins, 1993.

Foster, Richard J. *Celebration of Discipline: The Path to Spiritual Growth*. New York: HarperCollins, 1998.

———. *Prayer: Finding the Heart's True Home*. New York: HarperCollins, 1992.

The HarperCollins Study Bible: New Revised Standard Version. Edited by Wayne A. Meeks. New York: HarperCollins, 1993.

For Additional Reading

Merton, Thomas. *Contemplative Prayer*. New York: Image, 1996.

———. *Thoughts in Solitude*. Boston: Shambhala, 1958.

Mother Teresa. *Mother Teresa, Come Be My Light: The Private Writings of the "Saint of Calcutta."* Edited and Commentary by Brian Kolodiejchuk, M. C. New York: Doubleday, 2007.

Nesser, Joann. *Journey into Reality: Through Prayer and God-Centeredness*. Prior Lake, MN: Living Waters, 1998.

Norris, Kathleen. *Amazing Grace: A Vocabulary of Faith*. New York: Riverhead, 1998.

———. *The Cloister Walk*. New York: Riverhead, 1996.

Nouwen, Henri J. M. *Here and Now: Living in the Spirit*. New York: Crossroad, 1994.

———. *Out of Solitude*. Notre Dame, IN: Ave Marie, 2004.

———. *Seeds of Hope—A Henri Nouwen Reader*. Edited by Robert Durback. New York: Image, 1997.

Willard, Dallas. *The Spirit of the Disciples: Understanding How God Changes Lives*. New York: HarperCollins, 1988.

Tillich, Paul. *Dynamics of Faith*. New York: HarperCollins, 1957.

www.ingramcontent.com/pod-product-compliance
Lightning Source LLC
Chambersburg PA
CBHW060416090426
42734CB00011B/2340